Innovative Discoveries for Ecumenical Ministries

Volume III

A Narrative Tour for Pastoral Reform

Richard H. Guerrette

*To Eleanor Fanelli and Family
Toward Expanding
The Ecumenical Ministries
of
Pope Francis*

Richard H. Guerrette

University Press of America,® Inc.
Lanham • Boulder • New York • Toronto • Plymouth, UK

Copyright © 2016 by University Press of America,® Inc.
4501 Forbes Boulevard, Suite 200, Lanham, Maryland 20706
UPA Acquisitions Department (301) 459-3366

Unit A, Whitacre Mews, 26-34 Stannary Street,
London SE11 4AB, United Kingdom

All rights reserved
Printed in the United States of America
British Library Cataloguing in Publication Information Available

Library of Congress Control Number: 2015952283
ISBN: 978-0-7618-6685-5 (cloth : alk. paper)—ISBN: 978-0-7618-6686-2 (electronic)

∞™ The paper used in this publication meets the minimum requirements of American National Standard for Information Sciences Permanence of Paper for Printed Library Materials, ANSI/NISO Z39.48-1992.

Contents

Foreword	v
Preface	vii
1 **Identity Crisis of the Priest**	1
Pastoral Considerations of the Crisis	2
Organizational Analysis of the Crisis	4
An Ecumenical Discovery for the Priesthood	5
Summary and Conclusion	6
Notes	7
2 **Re-identity through Pastoral Reform**	9
Interdisciplinary Perspectives	10
A Sociology for Pastoral Reform	11
An Ecclesiology for Christian Ministry	13
Summary and Conclusion	16
Notes	17
3 **A Reformational Identity for the Priest**	19
Redefining the Role of the Priest	20
Ministries of Reconciliation	23
Promoting the Ecumenical Growth of the Priest	29
Summary and Conclusion	30
Notes	31
4 **A Sociological Plan for Pastoral Reform**	35
A Sociological Analysis	35
The Sociological Plan	39
Models of Structural Adaptation	39
Models of Goal Substitution	47

	Models for Respecting Latent Religious Values	49
	Models of Integration	52
	Evaluation of the Plan	54
	Summary and Conclusion	56
	Notes	57
5	Innovative Projections toward Ecumenical Ministries	61
	Ministry and Ecclesiology	62
	Ministry and Ecumenism	72
	Summary and Conclusion	77
	Notes	78

References	81
Author and Subject Index	85

Foreword

That there is a theological Crisis in the church—Catholic and Protestant—is now obvious. That the suddenness of its onset in the post-Vatican Council Catholic Church has created a special problem for Catholic priests is also apparent. "Openness to the world" after all is two-sided. It makes possible renewed dialogue with the modern spirit and intensifies concern for relating the Christian faith to the acute needs of modern spirit and intensifies concern for relating the Christian faith to the acute needs of modern man. That is gain. But it also reduces the traditional sense of mystery, of representing the transcendent, the holy, that was associated with priesthood. We can argue that this sense of mystery was no longer directly related to contemporary life—that it was nostalgic in its ebbing power. That is probably true. But until the dialogue of the faith with contemporary life leads to a new sense of the transcendent, we will necessarily face a sense of deep loss.

Father Guerrette seeks to work through this sense of loss, seeking to uncover paths that carry promise of the rediscovery of the role of the priesthood by pointing to the transcendent. He believes that such paths are likely to be found where the discipline of theology takes seriously the discipline of sociology and administrative science. By understanding the relation of the theological crisis in the church to the organizational crisis of the church, we will be in a better position to plan for the future of the church's mission.

His analysis deals directly with the Catholic form of the crisis. It explores the inner church situation in the post-Vatican Council period. Then with the help of the tools of social science he makes some preliminary proposals for the directions which the church should take. There is no way back except the way forward; and that way requires the courage of the explorer.

As a Protestant I discovered that while the analysis of the problem reveals differences in timetable between our previously separated Christian confessions, the differences are fast disappearing. We are being thrown together in a common crisis. Let us hope that we will find each other in the common task of finding the faithful path into God's future.

Colin W. Williams
Dean, Yale Divinity School

Foreword

That there is a theological Crisis in the church—Catholic and Protestant—is now obvious. That the suddenness of its onset in the post-Vatican Council Catholic Church has created a special problem for Catholic priests is also apparent. "Openness to the world" after all is two-sided. It makes possible renewed dialogue with the modern spirit and intensifies concern for relating the Christian faith to the acute needs of modern spirit and intensifies concern for relating the Christian faith to the acute needs of modern man. That is gain. But it also reduces the traditional sense of mystery, of representing the transcendent, the holy, that was associated with priesthood. We can argue that this sense of mystery was no longer directly related to contemporary life—that it was nostalgic in its ebbing power. That is probably true. But until the dialogue of the faith with contemporary life leads to a new sense of the transcendent, we will necessarily face a sense of deep loss.

Father Guerrette seeks to work through this sense of loss, seeking to uncover paths that carry promise of the rediscovery of the role of the priesthood by pointing to the transcendent. He believes that such paths are likely to be found where the discipline of theology takes seriously the discipline of sociology and administrative science. By understanding the relation of the theological crisis in the church to the organizational crisis of the church, we will be in a better position to plan for the future of the church's mission.

His analysis deals directly with the Catholic form of the crisis. It explores the inner church situation in the post-Vatican Council period. Then with the help of the tools of social science he makes some preliminary proposals for the directions which the church should take. There is no way back except the way forward; and that way requires the courage of the explorer.

As a Protestant I discovered that while the analysis of the problem reveals differences in timetable between our previously separated Christian confessions, the differences are fast disappearing. We are being thrown together in a common crisis. Let us hope that we will find each other in the common task of finding the faithful path into God's future.

Colin W. Williams
Dean, Yale Divinity School

Preface

Like the priest, a good social researcher is one who *serves* those whom he studies. However precise the quality of his data and however scholarly these have been compiled and collated with theory, his work is really in vain unless it is directed toward the improvement of the more humane living or working conditions of his subjects. All too often social researchers have conducted their work in a most unsocial manner, draining their respondents for data through questionnaires and surveys, formulating conclusions and even predicting outcomes without offering any concrete proposals for effecting social change.

Without prejudice to those who have heretofore engaged themselves in research studies on priests, one sometimes wonders whether their lengthy reports have been undertaken with sufficient circumspection into the identity crisis of their subjects as to render them service. Their data have been precise, their questionnaires and surveys, extensive; but priests remain drained and many disconcerted over the unheeded conclusions and the unfulfilled predictions of their studies. While these researchers are certainly not to blame for the failure of the church to implement their recommendations, their efforts were simply not conducted with a view to resolving the crisis through any concrete, practical proposal for effecting pastoral change. Thus, as scholarly as much of this research has been, it has not served priests very well.

As a parish priest involved in socio-religious research, I have attempted in this work to serve those whom I have studied by suggesting such a proposal as a means to resolving the identity crisis in the priesthood. Utilizing some of the precise data of my research associates on the work experiences and career growth of priests and interrelating this material with some organizational theory and a theology of ministry, I have presented this research as a working base on which an integrative sociological plan for the pastoral reform of the church has been constructed with the specific purpose of laying an ecclesiological foundation on which priestly re-identity can be built. From this ecclesiological base, I have formulated some theological constructs for redefining the role of the priest in a plural world and for rebuilding his career in an ecumenical church as the primary prerequisites for his new identity. With such a concrete plan for effecting pastoral change, the church can begin to implement the suggested recommendations for the re-identity of the priest. Thus, as practical as this research is designed to be, it can serve priests very well.

In a search for priestly re-identity, however, more is needed than sociological models and theological constructs for the organizational church. The rebuilding process must involve the priest himself, projecting him toward new heights that rise above institutional structures and clerical forms. For this reason, I have submitted some projections for the priesthood that focus toward an ecumenical ministry. These projections are intended to open the priest to a path of discovery on which he can develop some incentives for searching beyond what he has known and experienced and where he can subsequently find himself in a common quest for ministerial identity not only with his ordained Protestant and Orthodox colleagues but with every Christian.

Accordingly, this contemporary updated edition of *A New Identity for the Priest,* first published in the Paulist Press in 1973, is intended to re-configure the ecclesiological structures of the church with contemporary models of ministry beyond the MBO (Management by Objectives) diocesan boundaries of parochial ministry to the MBE (Management by Ethics) ecumenical ministries, as inspired by the roots of functional sociology of Talcott Parsons, and the innovative ecumenical ministries, as inspired by my symbolic interactional *praxis* theories (see Guerrette, 2015 Volume 1) and ecological *aesthetic* theories in Volume 2 with a *transcendental* Gallery Tour through the Corporate Moral Forest (Guerrette, 2015).

So, transcending one's accustomed ranges of parochial ministry involves a certain fear of the unknown and that is risk; but it also involves a certain *faith* in one's mission and that is *grace.* Jeremiah taught us this. When this prophet acknowledged the risk of his call to the nations and responded to the grace of its ecumenical mission, he found his identity in the *prophetic ministry* (1:4-19). When the priest acknowledges the risks of his call to serve a universal world and responds to the grace of its ecumenical mission, he will re-discover his identity in an *ecumenical ministry.*

In response to the grace of this ecumenical mission, I founded EquiPax as a Corporate Retreat Center for Chief Executive Officers with a Gallery Chapel for their aesthetic exposure to *innovations for Environmental and Corporate Art* and for their associate colleagues of corporate education in their corporate programs for Human Resource training. With this graceful spiritual mission, I have assigned my devoted academic successors, Daniel Robinson, C.P.L.C. and Barbara Robinson, D.A. from Harvard University, as contemporary *praxis* scholars to conduct the corporate retreat mission. The interdisciplinary academic breadth of their scholarly knowledge and the interpersonal aesthetic spheres of their own artistic and sculptural compositions will continue to provide this retreat mission for corporate executives and academic internship programs for graduate students from Yale Divinity School and the Schools of Organization Management and Forestry Environmental Studies at Yale.

Finally, *in memory* of my original scholarly associates at the Ecumenical Continuing Education Center at Yale, I would also like to acknowledge all my relatives, friends and associates who have helped to allay the fears in the risks I have had to assume in my own search for priestly re-identity: My father and mother, who have themselves responded to the grace of change; my sister Nancy, roster artist the EquiPax Gallery and her husband John Bandy, who, with their children Jaa and Joann, are themselves transcending their accustomed level of faith with the courage of a Jonathan Livingston Seagull; John and Catherine Lovrin, whose communion has kept me alive through the costs of discipleship; my faithful friends and associates Fathers James Fanelli of the Hartford Archdiocesan School Office and Pierre Minard, O.S.B., of the Hermitage of La Grand Foret in St. Aulaye, France, whose constant professional and prayerful support has been sustaining; Professor George Lindbeck, Father Henri Nouwen, Dean Colin Williams and Associate Dean Harry Adams of Yale Divinity School, who have been supportive sources of direction and encouragement; Professors Douglas Hall of York University in Toronto and Benjamin Schneider of the University of Maryland, who graciously conducted the appointments of the Archdiocesan priest studies and intensely compiling their research data at the Department of Administrative Sciences of Yale University; Professor John Koval of the Department of Sociology of the University of Notre Dame, Brother Didier Piveteau, Professor of Catechesis and Education at the Institut Catholique de Paris and Father Richard McBrien of the Department of Theology at Boston College, who read parts of the manuscript; Professor Raymond Bradt of the Department of Religious Studies at the University of Virginia, whose perceptive insights helped to open my vision to new horizons; and Victor and Ilke Loefflath Ehly, Thomas and Ruth Hummel, Professor Roland Bainton and all my other colleagues and our alumni of the Ecumenical Continuing Education Center at Yale who have contributed significant constructive feedback in the development of my ecumenical theories.

With graceful memories of our devoted ministries, I am most grateful to my brothers and sisters of the *Emmanuel Servant Community* in the parishes of St. John's Church in Watertown, Connecticut and the Church of the Nativity in Bethlehem, Connecticut and all the successive cooperative priests from the Archdiocese of Hartford who have helped them to re-identify in their lay missionary apostolate. Their trusted love and devotion have inspired me with burning incentives to record in this book our common experiences toward *an ecumenical ministry.*

Ecumenical Continuing Education Center at Yale
New Haven, Connecticut

Chapter One

Identity Crisis of the Priest

While the church had organized through medieval centuries its priesthood into hierarchical systems of clerical ministers for multiple theological and historical reasons, it had not provided its priests with adequate organizational resources to promote their psychological success and career growth in the ministry. Priests have not ordinarily been assigned to positions where their human rights have been so respected as to allow for their personal development in the priesthood. In multiple assignments, neither have they been permitted to function in their positions so as to fulfill their duties through professional collaboration in the ministry. Their personal dignity had been commonly violated by their having been impeded from acting freely and responsibly in their assignments. In such organizational conditions, which have developed from unfavorable authority relationships with their superiors, many priests have lost their ministerial identity.

Since the promulgation of the decrees of the Second Vatican Council which have called for signification changes in the role of the priest in the modern world,[1] scores of priests, anxious to reclaim their dignity and to reform their identity, are still exploring for innovative methodologies toward implementing these changes in the particular situations of their work assignments.

It is the purpose of this book to respond to priests who are still waiting for engaging in interpersonal and meaningful interactional ministry by providing more abundant pastoral resources through which they can acquire social psychological success to grow in the ministry and to re-identify their personal charismatic *leadership* role in the priesthood. This response must begin by briefly reviewing some pertinent historical pastoral research considerations of the identity crisis in the priesthood requiring *reconciliation* of the hierarchical authority structures which have impaired authentic Christological pastoral leadership for decades. With organizational studies of traditional Management by Objective MBO paradigm research conducted in 1969 by the Yale School of Administrative Science in which this author had participated, as a respondent, it had been clearly evident, at that time, that the organizational hierarchical church required pastoral *leadership* reform toward *reconciling* clerical dissatisfaction among younger priests and *re-building* ministerial identities in that pre-Vatican II historical period.

The literary research mission of this historical respondent, is now focused on re-analyzing the MBO organizational causes of that period toward reconstructing the contemporary Church of 2015 through the MBE paradigm of *Management by Ethics* (see Guerrette 2015). This active provisionary mission projects an innovative focus on interactional liturgical models of neighborhood communities along with the ecumenical hierarchical ministries of Pope Francis with his leadership model of reconciliatory re-building universal ministries with Judaic hierarchies and Orthodox liturgies.

PASTORAL CONSIDERATIONS OF THE CRISIS

Leadership. Having identified priests with the image of Christ, the Eternal Priest, by their sharing in his threefold office of preaching His Gospel, celebrating His mysteries, and ministering pastoral care to His followers, the Council had promised them the role of *leadership* of a Christian community based on a renewed relationship to authority:

> Priests, prudent co-operators with the episcopal order as well as its aids and instruments, are called to serve the People of God. They constitute one priesthood with their bishop, although that priesthood is comprised of different functions. Associated with their bishop in a *spirit of trust* and generosity, priests make him present in a certain sense in the individual local congregations of the faithful, and take upon themselves, as far as they are able, his duties and concerns, discharging them with daily care.[2] . . . Let them so *lead* and serve their local community that it may worthily be called by that name by which the one and entire People of God is distinguished, namely, the Church of God.[3] (Abbott 1966, *The Documents of Vatican II*, pp. 54–55).

In appointments where they are still required to serve under elder pastors, as their assistants, the Council had specifically instructed these older priests to create proper professional working conditions where the younger priests can express their ministry with *"trust"* and support. In the pastoral proclamations of Vatican II.

> Consequently, older priests should receive younger priests as true brothers and give them a hand with their first undertakings and assignments in the ministry. They should likewise try to understand the mentality of younger priests, even

though it be different from their own, and should follow their projects with good will. (The Documents of Vatican II, 1966- pp. 550–551).

Reconciling. The Council had also recognized the need for the innovative *development of new roles* for priests that are more consistent with contemporary culture and more productive for the mission of the church:

> All priests are sent forth as co-workers in the same undertaking, whether they are engaged in a parochial or supra-parochial ministry, whether they devote their efforts to scientific research or teaching, whether by manual labor they share in the lot of the workers themselves—if there seems to be need for this and competent authority approves—or whether they fulfill any other apostolic tasks or labors related to the apostolate. *All indeed are united in the single goal of building up Christ's Body, a work requiring manifold roles and new adjustments, especially nowadays.*[4] (Abbott 1966, *The Documents of Vatican II*, pp. 549–550).

It is regretful to admit that all priests are not united in the work of building up the Body of Christ. In the recently released summary of a sociological study on priestly life and ministry sponsored by the National Conference of Catholic Bishops, it was concluded that:

> Large number of priests are dissatisfied with the way the ecclesiastical structure is shaped and the way decision-making power is distributed; but the leadership of the Church does not share this dissatisfaction. Furthermore, it would appear that differences between younger and older priests on the distribution of power and authority are rooted in ideological differences about the nature of the Church and religion.[5]

Beset by an increasingly grave identity crisis, many younger priests waited well over twenty years before they were assigned to the *leadership* of a Christian community. They frequently became disillusioned in the ministry when they failed to discover the required roles through which they could have expressed a meaningful service to people that would have been significant to their own understanding of the nature of religion and the purpose of the church. Not only was their role statically fixed to subsidiary obedience but their vocational growth was impeded by authoritarian parochial structures that confined them to traditional assignments under dominative pastors with little or no opportunity for new adjustments. In far too many instances their role was ill-defined and their career under-developed because of unsatisfactory authority relationships and unproductive organizational conditions.

ORGANIZATIONAL ANALYSIS OF THE CRISIS

Subsequently, in a remarkably pertinent social-scientific study of the work experiences and career growth of Roman Catholic priests conducted by Douglas T. Hall and Benjamin Schneider of Yale University, extensive data had been uncovered that pointed to the underlying organizational causes of this crisis in role identity among assistant pastor curates. In order to properly analyze this crisis, it is re-constructively critical to read the data in the light of the theological considerations of priesthood roles and authority relations critically analyzed above.

By measuring the socio-interactional components of self-image factors among priest, the report revealed that:

> ... The curates consistently appear to be in a less favorable position than the pastors or specials. As a group, they feel more dissatisfied, more underutilized, and their self-perceptions suffer most drastically from superior-subordinate contacts... We view the criterion variables of satisfaction, self-perception and utilization of skills as indicators of the individual's level of personal development in his work. Therefore, we would conclude that curates as a group show a very low level of individual development, and we have seen that this low development is related to the type of authority they experience.[6]

By examining the characteristics of the role assignments of priests, the Yale study alarmingly exposed the scarcity of possibilities for the career growth of curates in the contemporaneous conciliatory period of the organizational system of the Vatican II church. The research acknowledged that "... it is a problem to a young priest that he has to wait 22 years before he can have a parish assignment with significant responsibility and challenge."[7] The following factors which inhibit the psychological success of curates demonstrate "... the great perceived underuse of the human potential available in the younger priests of the Diocese"[8]:

> (1) They possess extremely limited opportunities for goal challenge and work choice; (2) while most of them are prevented from working autonomously and from receiving any feedback on their work performance, very few enjoy *supportive* autonomy from their pastors; (3) they are frequently engaged in work not central to their concept of ministry; and (4) in such a work climate the possibilities for the attainment of their goal are considerably diminished.[9]

As a consequence of their study, Hall and Schneider conclude:

> ... the conditions necessary for career development through psychological success are generally lacking for assistant pastors in this Diocese, although certain of these conditions are present in varying amounts for pastors and specials. Therefore, we would indicate that there are many areas in which the

organization could provide improved opportunities for the growth of its priests.[10]

AN ECUMENICAL DISCOVERY FOR THE PRIESTHOOD

Building. This study impelled this author to act with an inspirational desire to commit my priesthood role toward discovering an *innovative leadership* of a Christian community in my own Archdiocese. Without waiting for 22 years, I assumed the role of the innovator. I sneaked out of the rectory home of the parish—not for an MBO census search for structural data on parochial membership, but for an MBE search for interactional parishioners—re-constituting pastoral neighborhood clusters of evening discussion groups throughout the parish within the larger nationally expanding organizational units of the Christian Family Movement, CFM. These mini-communal units in the parish of St. John the Evangelist Church in Watertown, Connecticut spread beyond this mother parish into its mission Church of the Nativity in Bethlehem, Connecticut, where the *Emmanuel Servant Community* was *born* with intercommunal Eucharistic liturgies celebrated within the pastoral boundaries of both parishes. (See Guerrette, 1981, for a sociologic doctoral study of an innovative floating parish.)

After personally consulting with Richard McBrien and my ecclesiological studies in *Do We Need the Church?*, I was granted a scholarship by the Archdiocese of Hartford for graduate research in pastoral liturgies at the University of Notre Dame. Subsequently, as a Research Fellow at Yale Divinity School, I composed this original study of the *New Identity for the Priest* (1973). With some degree of "social psychological dislocation" relative to ministerial boundaries (Lifton 1969), consulting with McBrien inspired my reversal of his own question: *Does the Church Need Us?* (1969), the answer to which impelled a personal response that the church needs *Me* to *identify Myself* as an ecumenical priest! And so, while pursuing my doctorate studies at University of Connecticut with Dean William D'Antonio, Chairman of the American Sociological Association, my researching interests expanded into the wider academic zones of the Society for the Scientific Study of Religion, whose Presidential Founder, Paul Pruyser, ultimately and providentially inspired my Volume II composition of *Ethical Theories and Moral Narratives in Art: A Gallery Tour through the Corporate Moral Forest* (2015) with the late Professor Pruyser's Convention speech:

> I have discovered that exposure to great art, as in a museum or concert hall, often leads one, with or without the artist's or composer's intention to recognize corporate and historical associations between religion and art. These associations shape the idea of culture as an enormously old and large matrix preceding the individual and his family which legitimizes and reinforces the

personal associations by its dense network of corporate associations which have all become a matter of public record (1976, p. 2).

These inspirational words subsequently opened my ministry beyond the organizational structures of ecclesiastical boundaries, earning my doctorate at UConn in search of a career-long ecumenical vision toward pursuing innovative ministries with this *new identity for the priesthood*. This vision has expanded through the years since my ordination—still projecting "corporate and historical associations between religion and art" along with *reconciling* the ideas of MBO conventional cultures toward the MBE post-conventional cultures of new identities for an *Ecumenical Church*. And Finally, with the publication of Volume II, *I have discovered* that exposure to the liturgical arts and the ecological and environmental sciences have universally opened the ecumenical windows of the EquiPax Gallery, as historically and inspirationally motivated by the Documents of Vatican II and their contemporary significance, for the pastoral care of the world through the *ecumenical ministry of Art:*

> In pastoral care, appropriate use must be made not only of theological principles, but also of the findings of the secular sciences, especially of psychology and sociology. Thus the faithful can be brought to live the faith in a more thorough and mature way.
>
> Literature and the arts are also, in their own way, of great importance to the life of the Church. For they strive to probe the unique nature of man, his problems, and his experiences as he struggles to know and perfect both himself and the world. They are preoccupied with revealing man's place in history and in the world, with illustrating his miseries and joys, his needs and strengths, and with foreshadowing a better life for him. Thus they are better able to elevate human life as it is expressed in manifold forms, depending on time and place.
>
> Efforts must therefore be made so that those who practice these arts can feel that the Church gives recognition to them in their activities, and so that, enjoying an orderly freedom, they can establish smoother relations with the Christian community. Let the Church also acknowledge new forms of art which are adapted to our age and are in keeping with the characteristics of various nations and regions. Adjusted to their mode of expression and conformed to liturgical requirements, they may be introduced into the sanctuary when they raise the mind to God. (Abbott 1966, *The Documents of Vatican II*, p. 269).

SUMMARY AND CONCLUSION

From this ecclesiological and organizational analysis of the identity crisis of the priest, it is indeed clear that his re-identity can only be re-established through the reform of parish structures which will permit more satisfactory authority relationships in the ministry and more productive organizational conditions in the church. As such, the analysis specifics that this pastoral reform must provide the priest with the opportunities for: (1) exercising an early *leadership* of a Christian community in his ministry; (2) setting ministerial goals for himself and for an ecumenical church by participating in the selection options for his appointment to an appropriate assignment where he can work to attain them; (3) enjoying autonomy in *building* ecumenical incentives through *reconciliatory* authority relationships; (4) being engaged in work that is central to his academic and practical concept of ministry; and (5) receiving feedback on his work performance.

With the realization of these innovative opportunities, the precise theological constructs necessary for re-defining the role of the priest will be drawn and the proper organizational conditions necessary for his career development through psychological success will be established. In short, the re-identity of the priest will be secured where he can experience and enjoy appointment options that he can choose in accordance with his own personality traits and charismatic gifts that would be conducive to his spiritual life and appointment satisfaction.

Finally, it is historically significant that the original study of this new identity for the priest, reviewed over 43 years ago by Yale Divinity Dean Colin Williams in the Foreword of this book, affirmed his own historical projection of the critical need for a "way forward" promoting innovative Vatican II ministerial tracks toward a "new identity" for priests. With these historical reflections, it is promising to note that the final sentence of the study which projects the inspirational need for the revision of the priest's identity toward an *Ecumenical Ministry* was actually prophesized in its original edition (1973) with a charismatic foresight of the Pentecostal virtue of "hope" with "*Lux et Veritas:*" "This endeavor would constitute the subject of further research and would *hopefully* contain the material for a subsequent volume." It is therefore imperative for all readers and especially for scholars and students in their critical analysis of this ecclesiological study to historically assess and comprehensively evaluate the numerous References and End Notes of four decades ago, spanning the original study in the Divinity School and the Department of Administrative Science (the *Alma Mater* of the Yale School of Management).

NOTES

1. See for example, "Decree on the Ministry and Life of Priests," arts. 1, 8, 22; Decree on Priestly Formation," Preface and art. 1; "Dogmatic Constitution on the Church," arts. 28, 37, 40–41; "Pastoral Constitution on the Church in the Modern World," esp. arts. 43, 62, 75–76, 78, 91 in the *Documents of the Vatican II*, ed. Walter M. Abbott, Herder and Herder, and Association Press, New York, 1966.

2. "Dogmatic Constitution on the Church," art. 28 in *ibid.*

3. *Idem.* The renewed relationship to authority which generates the interpersonal association of trust and generosity between the priest and his bishop is based on John 15:15: "I shall not call you servants anymore because I have made known to you everything I have learned from my Father."

4. "Decree on the Ministry and Life of Priests, art. 8 in *ibid.*

5. *Study on Priestly Life and Ministry* (Summaries of the Report of the Ad Hoc Bishops' Subcommittees on History, Sociology and Psychology), National Conference of Catholic Bishops, Washington, DC, 1971, p. 65.

6. Douglas T. Hall and Benjamin Schneider, *A study of Work Experiences and Career Growth of Roman Catholic Diocesan Priests* (unpublished manuscript), Department of Administrative Sciences, Yale University, 1969, pp. 66 and 107. In this study, specials have been designated as priests who are neither pastors nor curates but those involved in extra-parochial ministries, such as in education, in hospital chaplaincies, etc. The conclusions of this factor analysis are corroborated by those of the sociological study which reported to the bishops: "The condition of the associate pastor (curate) is poor. Job satisfaction in this group, for example, is generally lower than that of unskilled workers. Associate pastors also do not feel that they have very good relationships with their colleagues" (*loc. cit.*, p. 66).

7. Hall and Schneider, *ibid*, p. 76; see also note 111 on art. 8 of "Decree on the Ministry and Life of Priests," in W. Abbot, ed., *op. cit.*

8. Hall and Schneider, *ibid.* p. 74; see also the data collected by Joseph Fichter on the work capacity of priests and the use of their abilities in *America's Forgotten Priests—What They Are Saying*, Harper and Rowe, New York, 1968, pp. 131–134. Fichter states: "One of the most important conclusions from the present study is the widespread waste of talent among the full-time parish assistants, and the consequent restlessness and dissatisfaction among the lower-echelon diocesan clergy" (p. 207).

9. Hall and Schneider, *ibid.* pp. 106–116.

10. *Ibid.* pp. 115–116. Compare these conclusions with those of Fichter who calls for a complete reformation of the organizational conditions of priestly work and for the professionalization of the priest as a career man. *Op. cit.* pp. 208–209. For an important sociological research study which analyzes some of these organizational conditions as they relate to the voluntary withdrawal of priests from the active ministry, see Eugene J. Schallert and Jacqueline M. Kelley, "Some Factors Associated with Voluntary Withdrawal from the Catholic Priesthood," in *The Homiletic and Pastoral Review*, 71:2–4 (1970–1971) 95–106, 177–183, 255–267. This study concludes: "The renewal of the Church is perhaps the single most important step to be taken" (p. 267).

Chapter Two

Re-identity through Pastoral Reform

Interrelating the data of the above social-scientific study of the work experiences and career growth of priests with the conciliar theology of the priesthood emphasizes the need to redefine the role of the priest through the pastoral reform of the church in order to provide for his psychological success and vocational growth in the ministry and so to secure his re-identity. Both the theology and the data quite forcefully show how the role of the priest has been *structurally* determined by the form of the parish. Heretofore, not only priests but all Christians, save those who entered the religious life, have had but one pastoral option through which they could express their faith and mission—and that has been through the local parish. In an age when life was relatively static and confined to restricted areas of space and time, this territorial or geographical model was sufficiently expressive of a denominational Christian witness and quite effectively specified a particular parochial ministerial role. During an age when life leaps beyond the provincial boundaries of space and time, however, other pastoral alternatives sufficiently expressive of a more ecumenical Christian witness are required which specify more secular and pluralistic ministerial roles. Thus, new *symbolic* adjustments for contemporary forms of ministry imply a primary necessity to plan *innovative* forms of parish community in a mobilized society where the priest can discover the required *interactional* roles through which he can render meaningful service to God's people.[1] Such planning for priestly re-identity through pastoral reform demands a depth of vision which can only be projected through interdisciplinary perspectives.

Chapter 2
INTERDISCIPLINARY PERSPECTIVES

Since the completion of the Yale study of the priesthood, the archdiocese analyzed above had not provided many areas in which improved opportunities for the growth of its priests can be realized. It had adopted a rather selective approach to the interpretation of the data and had concentrated on the implementation of the conclusions of the report in the area of personnel procedure of priests' assignments. In this area an important program in team ministry and co-pastorates were set up to address the problems of rank and file ministry and seniority appointments. While the program had cut back on the prolonged twenty-two year waiting period for the priest's assumption of responsibility and challenge, it had not allowed sufficient options for him in diversified ministries where he could have experienced his appropriate psychological success and career growth.

Projectively, therefore, it is important to uncover the pertinent underlying causes for the Hartford Archdiocese's failure to creatively respond to the Yale study. After considerable debate in the Senate of Priests and among the entire presbyterate over an interpretive report of the study conducted by a preliminary personnel board of the archdiocese, a very forward looking proposal for implementing the conclusions of the study submitted by this board was rejected. A modified plan for alternative assignments in co-pastorate teams under the supervision of a permanent personnel board was subsequently adopted and implemented. The resultant vibrations from this heated debate over personnel issues and parish reform were felt and continued to be transmitted to a confused laity of the archdiocese through the forthright reporting of the distinguished *Catholic Transcript* archdiocesan weekly. From these developments, it is evident that while the clergy of the archdiocese were disturbingly polarized, the laity was wandering in wondering perplexity.

With compassion for the bishops, priests and people of this archdiocesan church, however, it should be stated that their struggles during those changing historical times of the seventies had been disconcerting due to the lack of interdisciplinary research which could have provided for them new insights into these organization problems of ecclesiastical reform. Little or no work in that historical period was ever submitted on the significant interrelationship between sociology and ecclesiology as a theoretical and empirical base upon which to reconstruct the forms of the parish and to redirect the goals of ministry. While the Yale report and the other studies referred to in this book were indeed helpful and had been conducted with a high degree of scientific and theological expertise, they were not initiated with any formal attempt to interrelate the respective disciplines and certainly not completed with any pretenses of designing practical plans for parish reform. What is now needed in a more contemporary study of this kind is to recognize that the identity crisis in the priesthood is much more severe with the closing of seminaries and the shortage of priests throughout the universal church. The most beautiful Gothic architectural Archdiocesan Saint Thomas Seminary in suburban Bloomfield, Connecticut has been changed into a retirement compound for priests and bureaucratic administration offices for the church. Such an administrative crisis for the church will be resolved neither by the pure scientific analyses of statistical surveys and interpretive reports, however steeped these may be in the secular sciences of psychology and sociology. Nor will they ever be resolved by any doctrinal theological definitions of ministry, however steeped these may be in the sacred sciences of Christology and ecclesiology. On the one hand, scientific studies on the priesthood have consistently missed the marks of faith, hope and charity which inspire the priests to devote their lives in service of the corporate body of Christ, even when their psychological success may be low and their career growth obstructed. Statistics can never quite adequately measure these theological virtues and ecclesiological concepts that constitute the foundation of the priests' vocation to the ministry and undergird their determination to persevere in its profession. On the other hand, theological studies on the priesthood have ironically failed to acknowledge the humanity of priests in service of an institutional church; and this at a historical contemporary time when Christological studies had radically stressed an ecclesiological focus on the *sacerdotal humanity* of Christ. (See the studies of John L. McKenzie, 1966; Hans Kung, 1967; Karl Rahner, 1968 and Richard McBrien, 1968.) If these latter studies can admit the human condition of God's Son, contemporary studies must admit the human conditions of priests and the organizational conditions of their church.

So recognizing the need to apply some organizational theory to ecclesiology can be helpful on two counts. *First*, it can provide a sociology for the integrative pastoral reform of the church from which practical plans can be devised to create more productive organizational conditions for the psychological success and career growth of the priests. *Secondly*, it can outline an ecclesiology for an integrative ministry which defines the need for more satisfactory authority relationships in the priesthood and for proper balance between its official and charismatic ministries. Only from these interdisciplinary perspectives which view the practical personnel problems of the professional ministry in the light of a sociology for pastoral reform and an ecclesiology for Christian ministry can the role of priests be redefined and their re-identity refocused.

A SOCIOLOGY FOR PASTORAL REFORM

The social pathological problems of the institutional church, so acutely reflected in the case study of the Archdiocese of Hartford and in the indicated reports of the National Conference of Catholic Bishops, are widespread not merely in the American ecclesiastical scene but abroad as well. These symptoms continue to undermine the organizational stability of the church, threatening the very foundations of institutional unity and ecclesial community. To appreciate the seriousness of these ills, one has only to recall the division that has set in in the Dutch church, not to mention the thousands of priests who have left the ministry and the numbers of these who have even separated themselves from the church. In response to one of the most publicized examples of these departures, namely, the case of Charles Davis and his question of conscience,[2] Gregory Baum has recorded an incisive diagnosis into these socio-pathological conditions and has prescribed "...the introduction of new social processes which open the church to the Spirit and enable her to give up her pathological attachments to the past."[3]

While one can hardly question the need for such remedial measures, the application of new social processes to the institutional body of the church constitutes an intricately complex sociological problem which causes organizational reactions much the same as occur in the process of the organic transplants of modern medicine. Because of the biological laws of organic unity among the cellular components of a physical body, any addition of a foreign substances into the body tends to be immediately rejected. Likewise, because of the sociological laws of social cohesion among the individual groups and successive generations of an *institutional body,* any addition of a new social process into the organizational life of that body *also tends to be immediately rejected.* It is not easy for anybody, physical or moral, to give up attachments to the past, even if these attachments are pathological.

In psychology, Erik Erikson points to the problems of the adaptive process in individuals growing up in society confronted with personal and social change. Recognizing the evolutionary levels of life and growth, he reflects a profound respect for history, as he plots the course of the individual's life stages and resolves personal identity crises through the preservation of "ego integrity." He maintains that one does not really give up his past even if it has been pathological; on the contrary, one builds and rebuilds his life from one stage to another and develops his potentialities while possessing the integrity of his life cycle, as he interacts with a widening social radius.[4] Applying Erikson's theories to institutions as well as to persons means that organizations and people all have an integrity of life whose order and meaning in history demand the acceptance of its past; and that when this past has experienced a pathological fallout, a new stage can be reconstructed upon its "essential strengths." Erickson's model draws a blueprint of these "basic virtues" which evolve from stage to stage and appear from generations to generation, thereby providing social cohesion for people and institutions challenged by changing systems of human and social values.

In sociology, Talcott Parsons constructs an AGIL paradigm of evolutionary change for modern societies and institutions which signifies an *agility* for the integration of differentiated systems and sub-systems encountering the problems of process and change (see Guerrette, 2015, Vol. I, ch. 7, pp. 204–5). Sensitive to the threats of polarization in social systems caused by innovators who would insist upon giving up the past, he articulates that "…changes do not imply that the older 'residual' unit will have 'lost function' in all contexts of its operations."[5] He cautions the innovator not to neglect other conditional factors such as the past when introducing new processes into the system.[6] He states that the primary function of the societal community is to integrate the system into a collective organization with unity and cohesiveness.[7] Parsons' AGIL model allows room for the introduction of new processes into institutions and societies and, through "adaptive upgrading," encourages those who may be pathologically attached to the past to ascend to a higher level and healthier order of commitment. In effect, his scheme, like Erikson's, utilizes the "basic patterns" or virtues of the system to preserve and to promote institutional *unity* and *stability* in the process of social change.[8]

Thus, it is impelling that when one would introduce new social processes into the institutional life of the church, one does not insist that its members give up their historically institutional attachments to the past. It is critical that these attachments remain as part of the integrity of the church's life cycle and concentrate on its essential strengths in the process of upgrading its life to a higher level and healthier order of commitment. Linking these basic institutional virtues of the church through the historical course of changing times, this approach ties together the successive generations of Christians with their respective value systems. Any scheme for the pastoral reform of the church which recognizes these sociological principles of organizational theory will not only preserve the unity of the church in the process of change but will also suggest appropriate practical plans for the reconstruction of the parish as a means to create more productive organizational conditions for the psychological success and career growth of the priest.

AN ECCLESIOLOGY FOR CHRISTIAN MINISTRY

As the Yale report reveals that improper "superior-subordinate contacts" have marred the self-image of priests and have contributed to their low level of individual development, its data reflect a distorted ecclesiology of Christian ministry. It is thus apparent that more satisfactory relationships must be drawn between Priests and their superiors based on the New Testament concept and expression of authority. The urgency of this need is accentuated by the following disclosure from the conclusions of the sociological report to the bishops on the priestly life and ministry:

> There are systemic and substantial differences between bishops and priests on almost every matter we studied. In most cases, the bishops hold different points of view and positions than even the priests in their own age group. Given the disagreements over power and over appropriate reforms in the Church, these systematic differences of conviction indicate a serious and potentially dangerous "gap" between the priests and the hierarch.[9]

The kind of authority relationships which Jesus had in mind for the church was expressed by him at the Last Supper: "You call me Master and Lord, and rightly; so I am. If I, then, the Lord and Master, have washed your feet, you should wash each other's feet. I have given you an example so that you may copy what I have done to you" (Jn. 13:13–15). From this evangelical living model of authority-subordinate relationships, Vatican II reconstructed a theology of authority for the hierarchical ministry in terms of *service* rather than dominion:

> For the nurturing and constant growth of the People of God, Christ the Lord instituted in his Church a variety of ministries, which work for the good of the whole body. For those ministers who are endowed with sacred power are servants of their brethren, so that all who are of the People of God, and therefore enjoy a true Christian dignity, can work toward a common goal freely and in an orderly way, and arrive at salvation.[10]

By so redefining the nature of ecclesiastical authority and redirecting its expression through the principle of collegiality,[11] the Council also restored the New Testament model of the sharing of apostolic authority among the various ministries in the church.[12] In effect, this biblical redefinition of authority calls for the restitution of the fullness of Christian ministry through the collaboration of hierarchical and charismatic ministries.[13] Post-conciliar theology compels the church to recognize the radical role distinctions of diversified offices and charisms that are an essential part of the apostolic tradition of Christian ministry and episcopal authority.[14] These distinctions in the ministerial roles are crucial to the resolution of the identity crisis of the priest since they provide corrective insights into the faulty superior-subordinate relationships of the pastor and the curate and draw new lines for bridging the gap between the bishop and the priest through more proper collegial authority relationships.

According to most scholars, the presbyter-bishops in the New Testament were the elder overseers of the Christian community (1 Tim.3: 1–7; Titus 1: 5–9) and eventually assumed the responsibilities of collectively exercising pastoral care over the churches founded by the Apostles (Acts 20: 28–29; 1

Peter 5: 2–4). With the expansion of the church into new areas and the multiplicity of pastoral responsibilities, the office ultimately split into the hierarchical form of the monarchical episcopate (one ruling bishop) and the Presbyterian priesthood (his associate priests). While the office of the priest then assumed the pastoral responsibilities for the individual churches, the office of the bishop took on the apostolic character of overseeing all the churches. Thus, the leadership of Christian communities became exclusively associated with the offices of bishop and priest at different sociological levels. As such, the priest was never intended to function in the capacity of an assistant pastor; the assistant with the deacon from early apostolic tradition (Phil. 1: 1; 1 Tim. 3: 8–13).[15] The restoration of this important role distinction in fulfilling the responsibilities of pastoral care should help immeasurably to solve many of the present problems of the pastor-curate relationship.

Some of the problems associated with the priest-bishop relationship could likewise be resolved, were these role distinctions properly respected. In particular, analysis of biblical research quest conclusively shows that the contemporary office of the bishop is distinct from the New Testament office of apostleship and that, as such, the bishop was not intended to be an innovator in the church. The innovator was the missionary apostle who encountered new situations. Those charged with the responsibilities for the pastoral reform of the church would therefore do well to acknowledge the limitations of the present form of episcopacy to either make "new adjustments" or to exclusively control them.

Perhaps then it would be wise for Catholics to affirm explicitly, and not merely implicitly, that in the modern church some of the principal activities of the Pauline apostolate, especially as regards offering leadership to face new religious problems, have been taken over functionally by men and women who are not bishops but by theologians, by enterprising priests and religious who by circumstances are thrust into new situations, and by perceptive laity with their manifold competencies in the complexities of a modern diocese. The main activities of most bishops do not and cannot take this direction. They can meet their responsibilities, however, by properly consulting with those who are involved in theology, in evangelization, and in new apostolates. The continuation of these functions of the Pauline apostle is the responsibility of the church as a whole.[16]

This is not to say that the bishops should not have any authority over innovative experimentation; on the contrary, to respect the valid historical and theological developments in the authority of the episcopal office, it is equally necessary that the bishops exercise a collegial supervision over pastoral innovation in conjunction with well-prepared innovators, who may be thrust into new situations, and with qualified resource people from theology and other related socio-religious disciplines.[17]

Although the restoration of more satisfactory authority relationships for priests should help to reform their proper self-image and should help to contribute to their individual development, a more authentic ecclesiology of Christian ministry cannot be expressed without a proper balance between the official and charismatic ministries in the church. It cannot be denied that the ministerial role of priests, which has been briefly traced in the New Testament church, has been onerously overplayed since the balance of ministry was disrupted with the diminishment of the charismatic ministries of the faithful. While it is not within the scope of this study to uncover all the reasons why the specific charisma of the faithful have been relatively inactive for centuries, it nevertheless seems important to acknowledge that the major causes for the deactivation of their charismatic ministries are more sociological and political than theological. With the spread of Christianity into various geographical areas and the consequent development of the parochial foundation of churches governed by a monarchy of bishops and served by a presbyterate of priests, the clerical caste system of a hierarchical ministry was established. This system, of course, had evolved from earlier species of clerical ministry in hierarchic Judaism.[18] However, in post-Judaic Christianity, the responsibilities of ministry were expediently assumed by the hierarchy of the clergy for practical purposes. Christian mission then became the exclusive prerogative of ordained clerics for political purposes. Un-ordained Christians eventually became deplumed of their ministerial rights and privileges with the consequent silencing of their charismatic gifts.[19] With faithful so slighted, their segregation from the clergy in the missionary activity of the church has, in effect, divided the unity of ministry and has confined its practice to the jurisdictional limits of canonical orders and to their corresponding institutional forms and styles. Because of this distortion to the one ministry of Christ, clerical ministers have been impaled with an identity crisis in their profession and the church impaired with an organizational crisis in its mission. The resolution of these crises demands the resetting of the balance between the official and charismatic ministries of the church for the sake of restoring the ecclesiological integrity of Christian ministry.

SUMMARY AND CONCLUSION

Recognizing the need to apply organization theory to ecclesiology for the purpose of planning for priestly re-identity has provided a sociology for the integrative pastoral reform of the church and has outlined an ecclesiology for an integrative Christian ministry. As these interdisciplinary perspectives have illustrated the importance of preserving institutional unity in a changing church, they have also projected the need to create more satisfactory authority relationships for priests and to reset the balance between official and charismatic ministries. Upon this theoretical base, a practical plan for the pastoral reform of the church can now be designed as a means to create more productive organizational conditions for the psychological success and career growth of the priest.

And even more importantly, upon the ecclesiological Parsonian AGIL bases of balancing official and charismatic ministries, over and beyond parochial and diocesan boundaries, the basic psychological virtues of Eric Erikson's essential strengths of social cohesion and interpersonal values, collegial authority relationships of serving God's people will be restored. From these innovative designs, a redefinition of the multiple ministerial roles in the church can be re-formulated for the priest's collegial leadership mission in ecumenical ministries.

NOTES

1. While this study is directly focused on pastoral reform as a means of redefining the role of the priest and restoring the proper organizational conditions for his vocational growth in the ministry, it is acknowledged that the primary questions of pastoral reform are posed by ecclesiology-namely, what is the church? And what is the purpose of the church? In order to adequately relate this study to these questions, it is suggested that the reader consult Richard McBrien, *Do We Need the Church?* Harper and Row, New York, 1968, and Colin Williams, *Where in the World?* National Council of Churches, New York, 1963. Tracing the development of ecclesiology from biblical times to the contemporary period, McBrien questions the relevancy of a Kingdom-centered church in a pluralistic world and points to some new ecumenical directions for the secular mission of the church. Tracing the development of the parish from biblical times to the contemporary period, Williams questions the relevancy of the residence-centered parish in a mobilized world and points to some new ecumenical directions for the secular mission of the parish.

2. See *A Question of conscience, Harper and Row, New York,* 1967.

3. *The Credibility of the Church Today*, Herder and Herder, New York, 1968, p. 96.

4. Erik H. Erickson, *Childhood and Society,* W. W. Norton, New York, 1963, pp. 247–274.

5. Talcott Parsons, *Societies: Evolutionary and Comparative Perspectives,* Prentice-Hall, Englewood Cliffs, New Jersey, 1966, p. 22.

6. Ibid., p. 114.

7. T. Parsons, The System of Modern Societies, Prentice-Hall, Englewood Cliffs, New Jersey, 1971, pp. 11–12.

8. T. Parsons, *Societies:* p. 114.

9. Hall and Schneider, p. 65.

10. "Dogmatic Constitution on the Church," art. 18, in W. Abbott, ed., *op. cit.*

11. *Ibid.,* arts. 22–24 and the *Addenda,* pp. 97–101.

12. See John L. McKenzie, *Authority in the Church,* Sheed and Ward, New York, 1966, pp. 99–100. Although the doctrine of the collegiality was defined by the council as it pertains to the hierarchical relationship between the Pope and the Bishops, its application in practice in terms of the sharing of responsibility in mission extends to the whole Church; see "Decree on the Missionary Activity of the church," arts. 37–38 and note 97 in *ibid.* Insofar as the practice of co-responsibility in mission and in ministry embraces the whole Church, it faithfully represents the practice of collegiality in the New Testament Church; see Hans Kling, *The Church,* Sheed and Ward, New York, 1967, p. 410 and J. L. McKenzie, pp. 64–65. It should be pointed out that the practice of collegiality as extended to the whole Church "does not mean that all the members of the Church have offices of authority, but that each member actively cooperates in the function of authority according to his own charisma." (McKenzie, p. 65).

13. See Karl Rahner, *Theology of Pastoral Actions*, Herder and Herder, New York, 1968, pp. 70–77. Hierarchical ministries may be briefly described as those *offices* commissioned by apostolic succession through official ordination to those called to the public services of the church; charismatic ministries, as those operations of grace given directly through special *charisms* or gifts of the Holy Spirit to individual believers for the service of the church (p. 73).

14. See H. Kung, *op. cit.*, p. 417. For a detailed description of the biblical nature, forms and functions of the various offices and charisms of ministry and their historical development in the church, see pp. 363–444.

15. See *ibid.*, pp. 409–413. On the specific role distinction of the deacon as assistant to the priest as well as to the bishop, see *The Jerusalem Bible,* Doubleday, Garden City, New York, 1966, Titus, 1 note b and John Macquarrie, *Principles of Christian Theology,* Schribner's, New York, 1966, p. 385. In the context of the liturgy, the role distinction between the priest as leader and the deacon as assistant is vividly illustrated in *The Apostolic Tradition of St. Hippolytus,* ed., Gregory Dix, S P C K, London, 1968 (an early third century document of liturgical texts). In this ritual, the priest is described as one who is ordained to "govern" God's people (8); the deacon, as one who is ordained "for the service of the bishop" (9). Throughout these texts, the deacon appears as an assistant to the bishop and to the priest; see, for example, 4, 21, and 23.

16. Raymond E. Brown, *Priest and Bishop: Biblical Reflections,* Paulist Press, New York, 1970, pp. 77–78.

17. See J. Fichter, *op. cit.*, pp. 203–204. For the bishop to properly fulfill his responsibilities of supervision pastoral reform, he must have access to competent consultants. He should therefore provide for the training of "enterprising" personnel who are professionally equipped to responsibility and creatively respond to new situations. In this context, see Edgar H. Schein, "The Role Innovator and His Education," in *Technology Review, 73: 1 (1970) 32–38.*

18. See Jean Danielou, *The Theology of Jewish Christianity,* Darton, Longman and Todd, London, 1964, pp. 346–356.

19. See George H. Williams, "The Ministry of the Ante-Nicene Church (c. 125–325), and "The Ministry in the Later Patristic Period (314–451)," in *The Ministry in Historical Perspectives,* eds. H. Richard Niebuhr and Daniel D. Williams, Harper and Brothers, New York, 1956, pp. 27–29 and 60–61 respectively.

Chapter Three

A Reformational Identity for the Priest

From the Post-Vatican II organizational climate in the church, it is restitutionally evident that the identity crisis in the priesthood has been evolving over decades and clearly demands that the Church needs more than a sociological plan for pastoral reform. What is imminently needed in this contemporary period of the clerical morality crisis of the priesthood's sexual scandals and the latent bureaucratic Curial scandals of institutionalized cover-ups is a *charismatic leadership* at the top of the episcopal and papal hierarchies. The latent structural-functional AGIL model of Parsonian sociology, presented in Chapter 7 of Volume I, is theoretically inadequate of resolving these scandals in what can be critically analyzed as a morally pre-conventional and institutionalized MBO cover-up of scandalous fear. The symbolic interactional post-conventional morality model of the MBE paradigm demands the integrity of honesty, especially in the hierarchical clergy and the managerial leadership at the very epitome of the papacy. Accordingly, it is providentially evident that the Holy Spirit of the Trinity has firmly and virtuously provided the papal leadership of Pope Francis to reclaim the dignity of the priesthood and the integrity of its ministry. His MBE leadership has opened the clarity structures of the Curia with an authentic paternal *ethos of caring reciprocity* for the victims of families and the weeping embarrassed symbolic structures of the penitential clergy.

It is providential to note that Gary Hamel, founder of an international management consulting firm in Chicago, has recently reviewed the exemplary management leadership of Pope Francis and has *providentially* and *practically* transliterated his own *praxis* corporate management interpretations of the Pope's reformational episcopal leadership message to the Curia of the Bishops and Cardinals:

Pope Francis has made no secret of his intention to radically reform the administrative structures of the Catholic Church, which he regards as insular, imperious and bureaucratic. He understands that in a hyper-kinetic world, inward-looking and self-obsessed leaders are a liability.

Last year, just before Christmas, the Pope addressed the leaders of the Roman Curia—the Cardinals and other officials who are charged with running the church's byzantine network of administrative bodies. The Pope's message to his colleagues was blunt. Leaders are susceptible to an array of debilitating maladies, including arrogance, intolerance, myopia, and pettiness. When those diseases go untreated, the organization itself is enfeebled. To have a healthy church, we need healthy leaders.

Through the years, I've heard dozens of management experts enumerate the qualities of great leaders. Seldom, though, do they speak plainly about the "diseases" of leadership. The Pope is more forthright. He understands that as human beings we have certain proclivities—not all of them noble. Nevertheless, leaders should be held to a high standard, since their scope of influence makes their ailments particularly infectious.

The Catholic Church is a bureaucracy: A hierarchy populated by good-hearted, but less-than-perfect souls. In that sense, it's not much different than your organization. That's why the Pope's counsel is relevant to leaders everywhere.

With that in mind, I spent a couple of hours translating the Pope's address into something a little closer to corporate-speak. ("I don't know if there's a prohibition on paraphrasing Papal pronouncements, but since I'm not Catholic, I'm willing to take the risk.") (*Harvard Business Review,* April, 2015).

REDEFINING THE ROLE OF THE PRIEST

The descriptive and evaluative speculation formulated from the framework of the sociological plan does posit a sufficiently broad base upon which the required theological constructs can be drawn to rebuild the image of the priest and to redefine his role. As a man of unity, the priest assumes an image and fulfills a role, throughout this plan, that faithfully represents the New Testament doctrine on ministry and creatively develops the teachings of Vatican II on the priesthood in the modern world. Reflecting these biblical and conciliar concepts, he is pictured as a *leader* of God's people commissioned by apostolic office to *reconcile* them to Him in pluralistic settings, *forming* them into His priestly people in a diversity of Christian ecclesial communities through His word, His sacrament by his own suffering service. Redefining the priest's role then involves three interactional functional terms of: *Leadership, Reconciliation* and *Building.*

Leadership. The leadership of the priest is closely designed in this plan according to the specifications of his pastoral office. It is thus distinct from but ecumenically related to the charismatic leadership of the faithful and encompasses the fulfillment of the liturgical, prophetic and ministerial functions of that office.

As a *liturgical leader,* the priest presides over the worshiping assembly of the community he is called to serve. Specially gifted by the Holy Spirit with a charism for leading worship and officially ordained by the Bishop with an apostolic order to express this gift for a local church, he acts as the principal liturgist for the community. In this capacity, the priest is to re-*present* the life of Christ to the community through the year and to direct the faithful in the celebration of His mysteries through the liturgical seasons. Inasmuch as the liturgy (*leitourgia*) is the public role of the people in its strict literal sense, however, the priest must continually strive to engage the people as a community in public worship in such a way that *their* liturgy is inspired from their own charismatic influence and bears the impression of their own authentic contributions and active participation. The particular responsibility of the priest, then, as president of the liturgical assembly, is to direct these contributions and to lead this participation so that the life of Christ and His mysteries unfold in a coherent and relevant manner through the celebrations of the church's calendar year. Thus, the priest should encourage the various forms of the liturgical community to assume their rightful ritual roles toward preparing the liturgy for common and festal celebrations under his direction.[1]

As a *prophetic leader,* the priest is commissioned by the Spirit and by the bishop to preach the word of God, *proclaiming* His truth to the community for its mission to society.[2] His leadership is to direct the community by his preaching so that his leadership image may always conform to its *biblical* Christological mission. This particular ministerial goal is christologically sensitive by *reactivating the role of Jesus* toward inspiring the charismatic influence of the faithful with their active participation in the liturgy. To this end, whenever other members of the community enjoy the prophetic charism to witness God's truth to society and to proclaim its message in and through the worshiping assembly, the priest should welcome this inspired involvement from his brothers and sisters in Christ.[3] However, since his prophetic ministry is charged with a collegial authority as well as with a mature spirituality and a developed theological training, his sensitively aesthetic expertise is to gracefully blend any critical political accents of his devout vision with his liturgical mission, especially where some "minor" prophets, like the Berrigan Jesuit Brothers, may *gracefully* color his message with their *prophetic* tones.[4] Within the community, this leadership is not always discharged with comfort, but it must always be expressed with love, for it is only through the common expressions of this charism that the order of men and the peace of God can be maintained (1 Cor. 14:32–33). Within the society, this leadership is not always discharged *sans reproche,* for it is not only the biblical record which gives witness to the rejection of prophets (Mt. 5:12; 23:34–36; 1 Thes.

2:14–16); it is also the juridical record that gives testimony to the fact that they are sometimes unjustly convicted as political criminals.

As a *ministering leader,* the priest is called to serve all of God's people in the community and in society as well. He is to respond to their needs, providing for their spiritual care, counseling them when they are confused, consoling them when they are disturbed and comforting them when they are sick. While his work in these areas requires the knowledge of professional training, it more importantly demands the wisdom of a *cultivated spirituality.* His leadership role as a spiritual therapist will be most effective when it is fulfilled as a suffering servant (Is. 42:6a-7; 50:4). As the Lord and Savior used His wounds to heal the sickness of sin, the priest must use his personal sufferings to heal the pains of people (Is. 53:4–5). Showing how ministry moves beyond professionalism, Henri Nouwen carefully opens this personal side of the priest, as *a wounded healer:* ". . . the minister, who takes off his clothes to wash the feet of his friends, is powerless, and his training and formation are meant to enable him to face his own weakness without fear and make it available to others. It is exactly this creative weakness that gives the ministry its momentum."[5]

This spiritual therapeutic process gains its greatest momentum when the priest interrelates the sufferings of all those to whom he is ministering and, in union with his own ascetic self, joins them to the suffering Body of the mystical Christ throughout the world (2 Cor. 1: 3–7). In this way, not only does he direct the faith and love of his brothers in Christ to universal realities (Col. 2: 1–5), but he projects their hopes to an eternal life in the risen Christ (Col. 3: 1–4).[6] Through this kind of spiritual corporate interaction the priest is sensitized to the needs of all those whom he meets and seeks to be an interpersonal friend and a personal agent of hope to them. Through the spirit of the glorified Christ, he is liberated to extend his missionary search for relevant ministering activity into unexplored areas of gospel service, which may involve "ordinary work" in the secular world. Fr. Nouwen challenges the modern priest to undertake these explorations:

> . . . more than ever it may be possible to experience the Spirit of Christ as—a living Spirit who makes it possible to break through the boundaries of our imprisoned existence and makes us free to work for a new world.
> But this way of the transcendental experience is a way that requires ministry. . . .It calls for Christians who are willing to develop their sensitivity to God's presence in their own lives, as well as in the lives of others, and to offer their experiences as a way of recognition and liberation to their fellow men. It calls for ministers in the true sense, who lay down their own lives for their friends, helping them to distinguish between the constructive and the destructive spirits and making them free for the discovery of God's life-giving spirits and making them free for the discovery of God's life-giving Spirit in the midst of this maddening world.[7]

Reconciliation. While the ministry of reconciliation is common to all Christians, the priest, as a man of unity, possesses special reconciliatory powers from the sacramental orders of his pastoral office. As in his leadership role, the powers of this reconciliatory role are expressed through the cultic, prophetic and ministering functions of that office.[8]

MINISTRIES OF RECONCILIATION

In the liturgy, the priest acts as the principal agent of reconciliation through his cultic functions of presiding over the Eucharistic mysteries, proclaiming sacramental absolution and administering sacramental unction. As a reconciling instrument of God's love, he administers the cup of forgiveness to the community of his brothers and sisters who, at times, from the human tensions of their gospel mission, break the bonds of unity in the fellowship of their service. As a reconciling instrument of God's mercy, he publicly announces to the community the forgiveness of God and the Church for any estrangement in the loneliness of sin experienced by the members.

Through the pristine historical ages, the sacrament of penance, as *personally private* confession of sin, eventually evolved within puritanically distorted ministerial cultures in the 12th century (Poschmann, 1963, Vogel, 1982, p. 213) as symbolically expressed in semi-closet-like confessional boxes, which subsequently developed into a ritually enclosed judicial systemic symbol of penance. This brief historical structural functional analysis of sacramental reconciliation practice still persists through the Catholic Church with little biblical nor liturgical authenticity and with socio-pathological undertows of residual guilt from psycho-historical waves of personal fears in para-liturgical atmospheres. Numbers of conservative priests and theologians continue to advise devout penitents and members of religious orders to access frequent confessions. This practice at times evolves into psychologically unhealthy over-examination of conscience and occasionally erupts with residually conscientious undertows of scrupulous guilt, impairing the sacramentally liberating processes of personal peaceful *reconciliation.* As a symbolic interactional reconciling instrument of God's compassion, the *caring fatherly pastoral priest* fully pardons their sins releasing all *residual pathological memories* within their personal conscience and re-unites them to the "mortal body" of Christ re-integrating the penitent through His cross (Col. 1:20–22).[9]

In the ministry of proclamation, the priest acts as the principal agent of reconciliation through his prophetic function of preaching the work of God. As the "major" prophet of the community entrusted by his pastoral office with the service of the Gospel, he preaches the apostolic word with reconciliatory power:

> It was God who reconciled us to himself through Christ and gave us the work of handing on this reconciliation. In other words, God in Christ was reconciling the world to himself, not holding men's faults against them, and he has entrusted to us the news that they are reconciled. So we are ambassadors for Christ; it is as though God were appealing through us, and the appeal that we make in Christ's name is: Be reconciled to God (2 Cor. 5: 18–20).

Commenting on this passage, Karl Schelkle describes how the prophetic function of the priest is efficaciously related to the ministry of reconciliation:

> ... God's action in Christ embraces both aspects, the reconciliation itself, as well as the depositing of the word of reconciliation. In this word God's reconciliation is now further actualized. By being addressed to the sinner, reconciliation is continually being achieved anew, and in this way the work of reconciliation comes to its completion...
> ... After Paul has said that the establishment of reconciliation by God is actualized here and now in the apostolic word, he says finally that the word of the apostle is the same as the word of Christ.... The apostle is the one who brings the word. But God reveals himself in the preaching and is operative in it.[10]

As the "major" prophet of the community, the priest fulfills his reconciliatory role of proclaiming the word in conjunction with the "minor" prophets of the community, the faithful, who, from their baptismal grace and charismatic gifts, possess a share in this role. It is, incidentally, precisely for this reason that the dialogue homily has reconciliatory efficacy. Since the reconciling power of the priest and the faithful is not limited to the cultic expression of proclamation in the homily, the priest, in union with the faithful of the community, works at the prophetic functions of reconciling sinners to God whenever he proclaims the word through mission in the wider community. Moreover, since the word of God may be proclaimed in a multitude of ways, the priest can, at times, be an effective agent of reconciliation, along with the faithful, by engaging in such prophetic missionary endeavors as marching in protest groups and fasting for peace.

In his ministering service, the priest acts as the conjoining instrument of reconciliation through the crucial labors of a suffering servant (Is. 49: 5a). By the ministry of his own cross, he reconciles people from the restriction of sorrow and pain, from the isolation of time and death and from the segregation of change and life, drawing them into an interacting convergence with the historical, the universal and the mystical Christ.[11] It is, moreover, only through this suffering service of the cross, which he must experience himself, that he can effectively respond to the problems of polarization within the church. "And when I am lifted up from the Earth, I shall draw all men to myself" (Jn. 12: 32).

But beyond the church, in contemporary times and within the secular domains of markets and money, as within the money changers in the Temple in Biblical times (Mt. 21;12), one efficacious way of drawing MBO money changers in the economies of scale in corporate culture and within the money markets of Wall Street is through the structural functional AGIL paradigm of Talcott Parsons, as critically and re-constructively presented in Chapter 7 of Volume 1 on *Management by Ethics.* This paradigm is ethically *functional* for reconciliatory building because of its paradigmatic efficacy of changing the economic system to meet the MBE needs of the socio-moral and economic environments (pp. 204–205).

Building. Redefining the role of the priest from the above models of Christian community in terms of building is obviously a question of redressing the administrative functions of the pastorate in its present role expectancies. However rooted and secure the church may be in a given place by the material structural components of a "parish plant," the role of the priest cannot be defined by any valid set of theological constructs in terms of the construction of parochial and ecclesiastical buildings. On the contrary, the interdisciplinary specifications drawn from the proposed plan for the pastoral reform of the church have set these constructs for building in terms of the *formation of a priestly people.* This role of the priest is likewise enacted and fulfilled through the liturgical, prophetic and ministering functions of his pastoral office.

From the liturgical resources of the church and upon its sacramental system, the priest is able to construct a "spiritual house" within which "the people of God" can abide. By means of the sacrament of baptism, he lays the ecclesial foundations of this *communal home* upon Christ as the "cornerstone" onto whom he sets the "living stones" of its inhabitants. By means of the liturgy of the Eucharist, he enables these believers, "set apart" in this *House of God* as "a royal priesthood," to offer "spiritual sacrifices" (1 Peter 2:4–10).[12] This kind of house building redefines the role of the priest as an innovative *community builder* charged with the task of forming God's people into diversified units of ecclesial worshiping communities, as indicated in the above plan. For example, in the latency or integration models of such a Parsonian AGIL plan, the priest could more effectively build Christian community at various demographic levels of the parish through an organized program of domestic and congregational liturgies celebrated to re-*integrate* the parochial unity of baptism and the liturgical community of the Eucharist. Preparing for and celebrating the Eucharist in small neighborhood groups where he would meet the expectant parents of the parish, he would be in a position to favorably dispose them and their neighbors for a deeper understanding of the corporate and ecclesial significance of the expecting forthcoming births of the children. He then could encourage the neighbors to take an active part with the parents in the preparation for the baptism of the children by anticipating some of the preliminary rites of infant baptism in the homes of the respective neighborhoods. By so involving the neighbors in the child-bearing joys of expectancies and in the baptismal rites of ceremonies, the priest would be forming ecclesial worshiping communities with familial domestic and neighborhood roots. In turn, he could place the living stones of the smaller neighborhood roots. In turn, he could place the living stones of the smaller neighborhood groups in the congregation by inviting the neighbors to accompany the parents and their newborn infants to the parish church to assume the honors of *communal* sponsorship. In this role as community home builder, the priest would interlock these groups as ecclesial communal cells for the larger parish community by means of a congregational celebration of baptism within a Eucharistic liturgy.[13]

Both in these cellular neighborhood ranges as well as in his parochial missionary fields, the prophetic voice of the priest possesses a reformative projection of the interpersonal and communal *Mystical Body of Christ* (Mersch, 1951). By preaching the word of God in the liturgy and by proclaiming its ecclesial parochial significance in his mission, he forms bonded inter-relational units of community among his believing hearers. This proclamatory function of the priest's prophetic ministry enjoys a sacramental efficacy inasmuch as the message actually effects what is audibly signified:

> Since the word as God's word is creative. . . , it does not merely demand what the admonition announces, but at the same time realizes it. . . .The proclaimed word creates the church not with a force that cannot fail, but only where it is heard and accepted. . . .The word creates for itself its community. It has its power from him and in him by whom it has been sent—and it still abides in him when it is released by him. (Schelkle, 1965).[14]

Thus, community building occurs not by means of a magical process but by means of a faith dynamic through the Holy Spirit. It is this same Spirit who, at providential times and proper places, moves the prophet to build community integratively and, whenever necessary re-integratively at the expense of condemning and reforming unserviceable structures:

> . . . valid preaching exists only in and through the church. Only where there is a church is the true word spoken and heard. Therefore, it may well be possible or necessary at some time to condemn and reform uses or abuses of the church by recalling the biblical word and using it as a norm.[15]

It is, of course, precisely through this above sociological plan for pastoral reform, which at times recalls the biblical word and uses it as a norm, that the priest can fulfill such a prophetic and integrative role as a community builder:

Thus says Yahweh: At the favorable time I will answer you, on the day of salvation I will help you. (I have formed you and have appointed you as a covenant of the people.) I will restore the land and assign you the estates that lie waste. I will say to the prisoners, 'Come out,' to those who are in darkness, 'Show yourselves'. . . . (Isaias 49:8–9). Look round about you, look, all are assembling, coming to you. By my life—it is Yahweh who speaks—(49:18, *The Jerusalem Bible*).

Finally, through the ministering capacity of an Isaian *suffering servant*, the priest works once more as an integrative community builder. Like the Lord, he utilizes his own personal sufferings to form the Church from his cross;[16] and so with Paul he can say: "It makes me happy to suffer for you, as I am suffering now, and in my own body to do what I can to make up all that has still to be undergone by Christ for the sake of his body, the Church" (Col. 1: 24). Commenting on this passage, *The Jerusalem Bible* states:

Jesus suffered in order to establish the reign of God, and anyone who continues his work must share this suffering. Paul is not saying that he thinks his own sufferings increase the value of the redemption. . . but that he shares by his sufferings as a missionary in those that Jesus had undergone in his own mission. . . .These are the sufferings predicted for the messianic era. . . and are all part of the way in which God had always intended the Church to develop.[17]

Developing the church as a community builder through suffering service is not a ministry prompted by a masochistic psychology of man but by an ascetic theology of the cross. It is this theology which enables Teilhard de Chardin to speak so positively of human suffering. For him the cross is not merely a penitential experience of expiation for sin but a constructive instrument for the mission of building the universe for God and of unifying all things in Christ.[18] (See the theology of Chardin in Volume 2 on the *Gallery Tour through the Corporate Moral Forest*, pp. 35 and 54.)

This creative ministry of Christ is discharged through the energy and force of love which inspires a priest to say with St. Paul: "Yes, I want you to know that I do have to struggle hard for you. . . . It is all to bind you together in love and to stir your minds, so that your understanding may come to full development" (Col. 2: 1–2). Ministering the cross to his brothers and sisters in such a positive and formative way, the priest can direct the spirituality of the community to its *full development* and thus enable its members to interact with one another in all their sufferings through the bonds of Christological love. Ministering to the needs of Christological love in human sexuality in contemporary eros cultures of the literary and performing arts is the greatest reconciliatory challenge for ecumenical ministries requiring the depicting of sanctity ethos cultures. (See the studies of the "moral sciences and the arts" in Volume II with the EquiPax Art Gallery themes of the *Holy Sanctuary of*

Love through the Music of Gustave Mahler and the Poetry of Wolfgang Goethe.)

As the above threefold re-identification of the priest in his ecumenical ministerial roles of leadership, reconciliation and building, he is inspirationally commissioned to reconstruct his biblical and conciliar identities, as a contemporary ecumenical missionary toward apostolic and liturgical service in a reformed church to a pluralistic society. Describing his image as formed by the liturgical, prophetic and ministerial functions of his pastorate and outlining his profile in the pastoral setting of charismatic ministries to the faithful, his commission projects these roles toward the *leading* of Christian communities, *reconciling* God's wandering people and *rebuilding* the sacred Body of Christ. This multiple role redefinition is further complemented by the lines of relationships that the priest enjoys with all of God's people:

> *Leading:* The pivotal principle on which the Council's teaching turns is that the priest is a man drawn from the ranks of the People of God to be made, in the very depths of his being, like to Christ, the Priest of mankind. He is consecrated by a special seal of the Holy Spirit. In virtue of this consecration, he acts in the person of Christ, and, as a minister of Christ, the Head, he is deputed to serve the People of God. . . .
>
> Bishops and priests, being united in their participation in the one priesthood and the ministry of Christ, although hierarchically graded, fundamentally are brothers. This brotherhood is not a mere communion of mind and heart, but is a sacramental reality. Its intimacy is especially close among the priests of the diocese forming one body (the one *presbyterium*) under the *leadership* of the bishop. . . . (Abbott, 1966, p. 527).
>
> *Building:* The priest is the minister of God's Word, of the sacraments and the Eucharist, and the *leader* of His people. All these functions find their "source and summit" in the celebration of the Eucharist. To form (*"build"*) a community, with a deep sense of its own identity, not static and hidebound by constricting parochialism, but open in love and action to the wider community of the whole Church and the world—this is the challenge the Council throws down to her priests. . . .(p. 529).
>
> *Reconciling:* The unity of action and spirituality is not achieved in gluing the external works of his ministry to his interior life by mere practices of piety, although, of course, they help considerably. It is Christ alone who fuses (*"reconciles"*) the two into one through the dynamic of a "pastoral charity" flowing mightily from the Eucharistic Sacrifice, "the center and root" of the whole life of the priest. Plunged into a diversity of problems and duties in today's world, the priest surmounts the area of tension between action and spirituality in the serene polarity of giving himself, united to Christ, in the service of his people (p. 530).[19]

Through the richness of building these relationships within which the collegial lines of authority are set and the integral balance of ministry reset, the reformational priest can recognize his new identity in a plural world through manifold ministerial roles in an ecumenical Church. What now remains is to examine how this Church is so reconstructed in its pastoral forms that it is equipped to shape the priest's new identity by promoting his *ecumenical* growth in the ministry through its more productive organizational conditions.

PROMOTING THE ECUMENICAL GROWTH OF THE PRIEST

The plurality of ministerial roles emerging from the rich diversity in ecclesial forms so proposed in the sociological plan does indeed equip the church for promoting the career growth of the priest as a means to re-shape his ecumenical ministerial identity. However, in order to accurately check the methodology of this reconstructed church for the purpose of determining whether the organizational conditions of its pastoral forms are sufficiently productive to promote the career growth of the priest, it is first necessary to recall the conclusions of the theological and organizational analysis of his identity crisis formulated in the above first chapter from the Yale Administrative Science study. These conclusions specify that the proper organizational conditions required for the career development of the priest must provide him with the opportunities for: (1) exercising an *early leadership* of a Christian community; (2) setting challenging goals for his reconstructive planning and for selecting an appropriate assignment where he can work to attain them; (3) enjoying autonomy in his work through renewed authority relationships; (4) being engaged in work that is central to his concept of ministerial studies and learning; and (5) receiving feedback on his work performance from parishioners and his ecclesial colleagues. In the organizational conditions created by these innovative plans for pastoral reform, the priest can projectively realize the following *re-creative* opportunities. *First,* in view of the widespread demand for specialized service in contemporary professional ministry and his corresponding specialization in training, as explored in Fichter (1968),[20] he can expect an early if not immediate, call to the pastoral leadership of a Christian community upon ordination, having fulfilled any needed requirements for pastoral experience in pre-ordination field work and internship settings. *Second,* with such variety in Christian communities and multiformative roles in priestly service, as proposed in this book, he can set challenging goals for himself in accordance with his interests and personal charisms and, through the services of a diocesan personnel board, select a suitable assignment with the approval of the bishop, where he can work to attain them.[21] *Third,* with renewed authority relationships based on the principle of collegiality and supplemented by an active diocesan personnel policy based on the principles of subsidiarity, consultation, competence, and cooperative planning,[22] he can be assured of enjoying a considerable amount of autonomy in his work by gaining the collegial support of his superiors and co-workers through cooperative and reciprocal interaction. *Fourth*, with the restoration of the collaborative relationship between charismatic and official ministries and the resultant role distinctions between their interactional forms of leadership, he can expect to be engaged in work that is central to his concept of the pastoral ministry. *Fifth*, through the diocesan structures of regional and parish councils, he can have access to channels for collective feedback in his work through the interactional processes of *collective discernment* and *collegial planning*.[23] In this kind of organizational climate where the priest can utilize his skills, enjoy satisfaction in his work and acquire adequate self-perception through his roles, he can steadily advance to a high level of personal development in his profession. In this kind of a *charismatic democratic church* where the priest can work to systematically attain his goals and thus periodically experience psychological success and sociological support, he can confidently expect to realize growth in his priestly career and so recognize a continuing development in his ministerial identity.

SUMMARY AND CONCLUSION

As the sociological plan for pastoral reformation traces the ministry of the priest through the liturgical, prophetic and ministerial functions of his pastoral office, it redesigns the necessary theological constructs upon which his priestly identity can be reconfigured and his pastoral role redefined. Tracing the priest as a leader, a reconciler and a community builder of God's people in each of these official capacities, the plan describes his ministerial work as integratively performed through the *leadership, reconciling and building* roles of his pastorate. Furthermore, it allows him sufficient flexibility within the organizational conditions of the institutional church to make the required adjustments through these manifold roles so as to realize his opportunities for experiencing psychological success and achieving career growth in the ministry. By so redefining the role of the priest and promoting his ecumenical identity, the plan not only traces his priestly profile in the ministry but actually inspires the organizational church to re-shape its reformational new image.

Inasmuch as the plan outlines an ecclesiological system for the modern church and its priesthood by developing its pastoral resources for constituting productive organizational conditions, it embodies for the church the kind of society that Pope John XXIII had in mind when he wrote:

> The society of men must not only be organized but must also provide them with abundant resources. This certainly requires that they observe and recognize their mutual rights and duties; it also requires that they collaborate togeth-

er in the many enterprises that modern civilization either allows or encourages or demands.

The dignity of the human person also requires that every man enjoy the right to act freely and responsibly. For this reason, therefore, in social relations man should exercise his rights, fulfill his obligations and, in the countless forms of collaboration with others, act chiefly on his own responsibility and initiative. This is to be done in such a way that each one acts on his own decision, of set purpose and from a consciousness of his obligation, without being moved by force or pressure brought to bear on him externally. For any human society that is established on relations of force must be regarded as inhuman, inasmuch as the personality of its members if repressed or restricted, when in fact they should be provided with appropriate incentives and means for developing and perfecting themselves [24] (Gibbons, 1963 Pacem in Terris, articles 33 and 34).

With its pastoral resources so abundantly developed by the specifications of such a plan designed from sociological theory, the church can indeed provide its priests with organizational conditions sufficiently productive to promote their psychological success and career growth in the ministry. In effect, priests can be assured of assignments to positions where their human rights are respected and their personal development fostered. In these positions, they can be encouraged to act creatively from the charismatic influences of their own pastoral purposes illuminated from their own continuing studies and their applied ministerial decisions. Accordingly, they possess a theologically grounded knowledge and corresponding practical (praxis) wisdom toward motivating their parishioners with responsibility for parochial and liturgical change. Enjoying the support of their superiors through collegial authority relationships, they can be inspired to collaborate in the ministry with their professional clerical associates and, together with them, can make proper adjustments in their ministerial missions to facilitate their Gospel roles of *leading, reconciling* and *building* God's people in a way that modern civilization demands. In such innovative organizational conditions, priests can, in fact, be provided with appropriate incentives and methodologies for developing their *leadership* roles and *building* Christological communities.

NOTES

1. With the reactivation of the charismatic influence of the faithful in diversified ministries and participatory liturgies, more cultic servers and readers will come forth from the people themselves, charismatically gifted to fulfill these roles. Heretofore, the ecclesiastical structures of the church and the canonical institution of the priesthood have all too often deemphasized the place of the Spirit in providing for cultic leaders. The institutionalization of ordination has marked the church with too many priests who do not know how to lead a devout and aesthetic liturgy. Obviously lacking the special charism for these purposes, they perform rites with such impersonal demeanor and perfunctory gestures that their only title to a valid priesthood is through orders and jurisdiction. However necessary this title may be for the hierarchical tradi-

tions of the church, it must be recognized that cultic leaders are not made by imposing hands or canonical documents. Nor are they bred by the impersonal ceremonies of irresponsive congregations. The special charism from the Spirit for leading worship is a fundamental prerequisite for any cultic leader and must be cultivated in the modern church by private prayer, by personal celebrations of responsive congregations and by professional training. As a matter of tradition, it should be remembered that in the early church, cultic leaders were known by their charismata (see J. Danielou, *The Theology of Jewish Christianity*, pp. 349–350).

2. Again, the relationship between charism and office is of equal importance to the prophetic leader. What is particularly significant for a traditional and ecumenical understanding of this relationship is that the prophetic leader in some parts of the early church was also the cultic leader. See 1 Cor. 14:29–33; the *Didache, X,* 7; XIII, 3; and the *Shepherd* of Hermas, Mand. XI, 7–10.

3. See Ernst Kasemann, *Essays on New Testament Themes* pp. 59–60.

4. See "The United States of America vs. the Berrigans: Some Documents," "The Indictment" and "The Response of 'The Conspiracy'" in *The Berrigans,* eds. William VanEtten Casey and Philip Nobile, Avon Books, New York, 1971, pp. 220–237, 238–244, 245–247 respectively.

5. Creative Ministry, Doubleday, New York, 1971, p. 110.

6. See Pierre Teilhard de Chardin, The Divine Milieu, Harper Torchbooks, New York, 1965. In this religious classic, the author lays a theological foundation for the process of spiritual interaction in Christian ministry from pp. 140 to 146.7.

7. H. Nouwen, op. cit., pp. 115–116.

8. For a clear discussion on the faithful's participation in the ministry of reconciliation and their relationship to the priest as leader, see J. Macquarrie, op. cit., pp. 374–382 and 388.

9. Colossians 1:22 "The human mortal body is that of his Son (lit. "flesh body"); this provides the locus where the reconciliation takes place. Into this body the entire human race is effectively gathered, cf. Ephesians 2:14–16, because Christ has assumed its sin, ...The 'flesh' body is the body as affected by sin." As also explained in 2 Corinthians, "For our sake God made the sinless one into sin so that in him we might become the goodness of God" (5:21).

10. *Discipleship and Priesthood*, Herder and Herder, New York, 1965, pp. 66–69.

11. See Teilhard de Chardin, *op. cit.,* pp. 102–104 and 115–117.

12. Notice how the formation of the faithful into a priestly people is described in this epistle in relation to their liturgical life, especially as regards baptism and the Eucharist.

13. For a more detailed commentary on the liturgy of infant baptism and on its pastoral celebration as a means to form Christian community, see Guerrette, "The New Rite of Infant Baptism," *Worship*, 43:4 (1969) 224–230.

14. K. Schelkle, *op. cit.,* pp. 74–75.

15. *Ibid.*, pp. 76–77.

16. Patristic imagery reflects this formative functions of Christ's ministry of suffering service by picturing Jesus as forming the church from his sacred side as he slept on the cross. See St. Bonaventure, *The Tree of Life,* no. 30 in *The Works of Bonaventure, Mystical Opuscula I,* St. Anthony Guild Press, Paterson, New Jersey, 1960, p. 127.

17. See note "m" in Colossians ch. 1:24 of *The Jerusalem Bible* which states that "Jesus suffered in order to establish the reign of God, and anyone who continues (H)is work must share this suffering." This shared Christological suffering is what the *Mystical Body of Christ* is all about. See the inspirational work of Emil Mersch (1951).

18. See op. cit., pp. 101–104 and Robert L. Faricy, Teilhard de Chardin's Theology of the Christian in the World, Sheed and Ward, New York, 1967, pp. 168–172.

19. Theology Subcommittee of the National Conference of Catholic Bishops, op. cit., quoted in loco cit., no. 4.

20. See Fichter, Joseph, (1968) *America's Forgotten Priests—What They Are Saying,* New York, Harper and Row.

21. See also E. Schein, *op. cit.,* pp. 35–37. Describing the style of contemporary professional work and its specialized roles, Schein illustrates the need for the professional school to prepare its students for the reality of specialization by engaging them in field-oriented team projects with ample opportunity for theoretical analysis through interdisciplinary research. He

insists that, in addition to the acquisition of their own particular professional sills, students be equipped with other skills in applied behavioral science. He urges, furthermore, that the professional school take an active part in guiding the early career paths of its graduates to insure the proper application of their training and the continued growth of their learning. His approach to professional education is sorely needed in seminaries (see Fichter, pp. 90–91) and could fittingly prepare priests with the necessary skills for their pivotal, relevant and peripheral roles of ministry in the service of the church and of society. (See note 16, chapter 4.)

22. In this regard, it is especially necessary to recognize a significant theological and organizational distinction involved in the selection of the priests assignment. While a variety of choices for ministerial work should certainly be available to every priest and while the functions of the diocesan personnel board are precisely for the purpose of systematically providing this variety through professional managerial procedures, it must be remembered that the priest's choice not only depends on his personal interests and professional competency but ultimately rests upon the New Testament concept of election by God to serve his people (Heb. 5:1–10). This theological dimension to occupational selection thus gives primary importance to the needs of the diocese and to the roles of both the bishop and the particular community to be served in finalizing the appointment of the priest. On the rights of the local community in this matter, see Hans Kung, *The Church,* p. 441.

23. See A. Greeley, "Principles of Personnel Policy," in *Secular Priest* in *The New Church,* ed. Gerard S. Sloyan, Herder and Herder, New York, 1967, pp. 166–175.

24. This right founded on the charism of discernment (1 Cor. 12:10; 1 In. 4:1–3). See H. Kung, *The Church,* (1967) pp. 421–422 and 440.

Chapter Four

A Sociological Plan for Pastoral Reform

In order to systemically design a practical plan for the pastoral reform of the church as a means to create more productive organizational conditions for the practice of ministry and for a new identity in its profession, it is critically imperative to more thoroughly analyze the social psychological and organizational conflicts which are contributing to the identity crisis of the priest. This more probing analysis will help to more analytically locate the institutional tensions in the church that have been demoralizing the pastoral spirit of priests while dividing and wakening their missionary endeavors. The analysis will also help to assess the threats of this polarization process provoked by some hierarchical and senior pastors, pathologically attached to the past, and by multiple younger and more liberal priests disruptively detached from its organizational history. Because of these functional problems of differentiation in the organizational clerical system of the church and the corresponding need for an interactional integrative plan for their resolution, the sociological theories of Talcott Parsons, briefly reviewed in the previous chapter as a structural functionalist theorist and relatively conservative sociologist of religion, are critically and practically suited to conduct the analysis and to construct the plan.

A SOCIOLOGICAL ANALYSIS

According to Parsons, the organizational conflicts of any institution can be adequately resolved by respecting "four independent functional imperatives": *adaptation, goal-attainment, integration* and *latency*. While an organization operates according to an institutionalized value system, it nevertheless is subject to constant external and internal pressures to change its values. These pressures arise from two primary sources of change, namely, cultural and motivational. The *cultural sources* are those which originate from *outside* the organization's value system and impel some members to adopt other values because of such external influences. The *motivational sources* are those which originate from *inside* the organization's social structure, giving rise to certain internal motivational tensions among some members to rebel against particular institutionalized role expectations. As these two sources of change generate the organizational conflicts of an institution, they, in effect, challenge the values of its "pattern maintenance" (structures) and its "tension management" (authority). Thus, the most important *functional* imperative relative to the organization's stability is the *latency* of its underlying historical value system. In the stress of these system problems arising from these two sources of change, the organization's efficiency is restricted and its institutional unity, resisted. As the functional imperative invoked to relax these strains, integration seeks to maintain solidarity among the diversified units of membership and to promote operational efficiency. The two remaining functional imperatives, adaptation and goal-attainment, are set in motion by the conflicts arising out of the organization's interchange with the external environment and its situational conditions respectively. The adaptive function is responsive to the problems provoked by the process of differentiation in the environment and enables the organization to grow as it encounters change. The function of goal-attainment permits the organization to control its environment by synchronizing the confronted situational conditions with its strategy for gratification.

This general theory of Parsons, usually signified as his AGIL scheme, shows how these four functional imperatives can maintain equilibrium in an institution and insure its continued existence and growth in spite of its organizational conflicts.[1]

Using this AGIL scheme of Parsons as an analytical base, it is possible to outline the organizational conflicts of the institutional church and to illustrate how its system problems can be resolved through *structural adaptation, goal substitution* and *integration* with respect for its *latent religious values.* While this use of Parsons' scheme assesses the internal and external organizational needs of the institutional church and measures its adaptive capacity for coping with the problems of social change in the external environment, the design is not focused on the church's "ability to change the environment to meet the needs of the system," as Parsonian usage would dictate,[2] but on its ability to change the system to meet the needs of the environment, as conciliar tutelage would indicate.[3] The church, unlike other institutions of society dependent on economic gratification from the attainment of their goals, exists for the disinterested ministerial service of society. As a social institution engaged in evangelization for the attainment of ultimate spiritual goals, it operates according to the principle of adaptation and therefore must change its system, whenever necessary, to include the substitution of more immediate temporal goals in order to insure its missionary gratification. The purpose of the scheme, then, is to construct a fundamental sociological framework for parish reform through which the church can acquire a more transcendent social identity in an institutionalized missionary enterprise.[4]

Structural Adaptation. As traditional parish structures tend to contain the church within the confines of its own residential interests, more committed Christians recognize the need to adapt these structures in order to maximize the church's relationship to the external environment and to mobilize its resources for the more mission-oriented goals of serving the distressed of society. With some already involved in adapted forms of Christian community, these believers frequently commit themselves to the apostolate within the organization through a variety of social movements external to the organization, and, if necessary, through the underground. In effect, those who remain within the institution are more often than not suspect of their liberal persuasions and labeled as "litniks" or "ecumaniacs." Those who are forced underground are isolated from the main lines of communication in the church or, at worst, separated from its fellowship by unofficial excommunication.

Goal Substitution. Because of the economic strain and institutional weight of parochialism and its self-containing goals, perceiving Christians are beginning to question the values of their attainment. As these people become more aware of the secular implications of the church's mission and more sensitive to the immediacy of human suffering and want, they begin to substitute more relevant goals that are capable of responding to the urgency of the situation. By engaging themselves in the civil rights movement, the peace movement, the youth movement and the like, they are determined to change the system, political as well as ecclesiastical, to meet the needs of the people. They are convinced that by adopting the goals of these movements they can be a more meaningful sign of *hope in the Eternal* to those struggling in the despair of the present. They insist that this sign can be most forcefully expressed through the socio-political dimensions of missionary goals. In effect, these Christians are often disturbingly dismissed as social or political activists and at times reproachfully condemned as "radicals."

Integration. Sensitive to the problems of the young and the old, and of liberals and conservatives, more moderate Christians prefer to work *within the system* to effect needed change. Careful not to disregard the latent religious values of their conservative confreres and cautious to apply the "adaptive upgrading" innovations of their liberal associates, these Christians are committed to preserve the unity of the Church and to insure its effectiveness in mission. In effect, though they may be in the best positon to bring about solidarity and efficacy in the institutional church through their integrative efforts, they are seriously handicapped by a lack of hierarchical support and leadership and by a need for a sustained and systemic plan for responding to change.

While the hierarchy of this country may be unresponsive to these organizational conflicts in the church, as one could safely conclude from the data uncovered in the above-mentioned reports and from the timely critical analysis submitted by Father Andrew Greeley, Chairman of the National Conference of Catholic Bishops' subcommittee on sociology[5], it should in all fairness be admitted that the bishops likewise suffer from a need for a scientific plan for responding to change in the church. One of the most familiar calculative political under-sights, that these bishops and others of the institutional hierarchy committed to the integrative structural functional imperative are misled by, is that *change in the system must be implemented gradually*. For an age characterized by the phenomenology of rapid social change, however, the slow implementation of change in the church can be disastrous. This fundamental point is beyond question and is well-marked by the socio-religious problems of racial and cultural alienation that have erupted in the church and in society. Slow change has cheated not only priests but all Christians and all people as well. What is needed therefore for the particularly pressing problems of polarization in the church is a calculative *sustained* and *systemic plan* for responding to rapid social and religious change *carefully* and *scientifically* designed to preserve the *unity of its membership* and to enhance the *efficiency of its mission*.

Latent Religious Values. Threatened by new forms of structural adaptation and by old fears of secularized goals, the more conservative Christians are stabilizing into their "protective" congregations determined to preserve their latent religious values. Older people, unable to relate secularization to their beliefs, tend to suspect church renewal, fearful of losing the continuity of tradition and their dependent religious identity. The Parsonian "pattern maintenance" function of the traditional form of the parish and the "tension management" function of the expected role of the priest relax the fears created by renewalists and protect them from the external pressures of cultural change. In effect, these Christians are all too often written off by renewalists as having nothing to contribute to the modern church and not too infrequently neglected by insensitive innovators who fail to transmit the *treasures of tradition* to the young. Clothed in garments of social change, the youth are consequently unable to relate tradition to contemporary lifestyles and counter-cultural values and are incapable of identifying in the dormant congregations of their parents. They are thus tending to abandon all institutional forms of the church, with some seeking new religious experiences through a variety of natural and transcendental means.

THE SOCIOLOGICAL PLAN

Incorporating the four independent functional imperatives of Parsonian theory into an ecclesiological design, the following *careful* sociological plan for the pastoral reform of the church is *scientifically* proposed to resolve its organizational conflicts. This plan is also presented as a means for creating more productive organizational conditions in the church toward preparing the setting for the integrative practice of Christian ministry. First, it should increase the church's missionary efficiency by providing a multiplicity of ministerial roles for the priest through which he can experience psychological success and career growth. Secondly, it should establish the proper conditions in the organization for the reconstitution of collegial authority relationships through which the balance between official and charismatic ministries can be reset. Based on the AGIL scheme of Parsons, the plan contains various specific models of parish community which are designed to effect the structural adaptation, the goal substitution and the integration of local diocesan communities of parishes with particular sensitivity for the latent religious values of older priests and parishioners. Four sets of models are described representing different forms of local parochial communities in a variety of mission situations. A brief delineation of the specialized role of the priest in each model set with an evaluation of some crucial functional aspects of the set relative to the ministry is also drawn as an outline from which conclusions can be formulated for his role redefinition and career growth in the priesthood and for his new identity in the ministry.

MODELS OF STRUCTURAL ADAPTATION

Employing the functional imperative of structural adaption, the following set of models would open the church to the wider interests of society and would maximize its relationship to the external environment. These models would expand the missionary activity of the church and would mobilize its ministerial resources to include the previously inactive charisms of the faithful. In addition, the forms of Christian community shaped by these models would attune the church to the Council's admonitions by engaging the priest in ministerial "work requiring manifold roles and new adjustments."

The Floating Parish. This form of Christian community would be based on the New Testament concept of fellowship or fraternal communion in Jesus Christ expressed as a "Way" of life (Acts 9:2, 18:25–26; 19:9; 22:4; 24:14, 22) in the breaking of the bread, in the gospel mission to society and in common prayer (Acts 2:42–47). By following this "Way," the members would realize strong bonds of mutual concern for one another and would extend this concern to the poor in selected areas of various mission activities.

In addition to serving the material needs of the afflicted, they would occasionally break the bread of the Eucharist with them in their homes and comfort them with God's saving word. They would also celebrate the Eucharist together on Sundays wherever the community might be engaged in a specific mission project. During the week, the members could follow the early Christian practice of offering morning and evening prayer in common when assembled for committee work or missionary assignment; otherwise they could so: Adapt this primitive custom as to observe it in private as a daily inspirational means of communal interaction. The membership of the community would be open to anyone desirous of giving witness to this "Way" of the Christian life. Its size would be determined only by the effectiveness of communication and collaboration among the members.

The Commune. With the advent of the new ethics and its emphasis on personal and provident responsibility through free and creative responses to human situations[6] and with the widespread changes in cultural values and lifestyles among the younger generation, some Christians might be called to give witness to gospel values in this context through a commune model. In this form of Christian community, the members would be enabled to enter into deeper interpersonal bonds of mutual concern, likewise based on Acts 2:42–47. "The faithful all lived together and owned everything in common" (v. 44). The members could express this "Way" of the Christian life in a semi-monastic style insofar as they would partake of meals in common and would daily observe specified hours for common prayer according to a convenient schedule. They would appropriately adapt this style, however, to contemporary social patterns of work and leisure and religious modes of worship and mission. They could, for example, frequently break the bread of the Eucharist together in their home and cooperate in various missionary projects through local community organizations. From time to time, they could participate in the liturgy of the neighboring parish and help with its apostolate. They could also enjoy membership in a floating parish or in other forms of community which might be complementary to their ways of witness.[7] It would be especially significant that these Christians express their "Way" of life openly both in traditional cultural areas and in counter-cultural settings. In the former area, the customary monastic expression of hospitality could be most effectively extended to local parishioners by opening guest rooms with invitations to participate in this "Way" of life for selected periods, a gesture which would immeasurably help to reduce immorality suspicion and to confirm the genuine character of such a *morally developed postconventional* style of the Christian life. (See Guerrette 2015 Vol. 1 Exhibits 3:1 and 3:4 ch. 3 pp. 60 and 80.) In the latter setting, a redeeming sign of the "Way" could be witnessed, through similar strategy, to some adherents of the counter-culture who are wandering in their search for authentic values."[8]

The Pentecostal Community. The distinct form of this community would be charismatic in the biblical sense of 1 Cor. 1:4–9; 12:4–11. Although charisms as gifts of the Holy Spirit are for the whole Church (1 Cor. 12:12–30), they would be regulated in this community through special meetings of prayer (1 Cor. 14:26–40). While these diverse gifts would be given by the Spirit for the inner peace and strength of the community (1 Cor. 14:26, 33), they would open the members to His power (Acts 2:1–13) inspiring them to build up the body of Christ in the service of the apostolate (Eph. 4:7–12). Inasmuch as the gifts would often be manifested by intense religious experiences, such as prophesying and speaking in tongues, they would require some spiritual direction and pastoral supervision, especially for the service of mission. In this regard, it would be wise for the members to heed the admonitions uttered by Paul that these charisms should always be utilized for the benefit of the community and the edification of the people (1 Cor. 14:3–5, 12, 19, 26).

Appearing as the conclusion of a lengthy discourse on the nature and purpose of these charismatic gifts in the body of Christ, these admonitions accentuate the importance of the community's preserving unity with the universal Church. For these purposes the place of the liturgy in the Pentecostal community could be most efficacious. Not only could the celebration of God's word and sacrament be an integrating ecclesial experience in worship; it could also provide the wisdom and the grace for cooperative involvement with the local parish in witness.[9]

The Servant Parish. In neglected areas stricken with poverty, racial injustice and other such social evils, the Church could obediently fill its biblical role as "suffering servant" (Is. 42:6–7; 50:4–5) by the formation of a community placed at the *service of the poor.*[10] Operating out of a storefront in a strategic inner city location, the community would be comprised of members inclined to express their Christian commitment through social work. A limited staff of full time social workers would conduct such necessary services as food collections, emergency housing, legal aid and referrals. This staff would also be responsible for enlisting volunteers from suburban parishes or from other communities to *serve* the poor as members of the mission.

The characteristic difference between this operation and other social service agencies of community organizations is that the servant parish would form a worshiping community. Its main purpose would be to convey a *living sign of hope* to oppressed people and to alleviate their sufferings. This, in conjunction with the social service activities of their mission, the members would frequently celebrate their hope in Jesus Christ through the Eucharist and other forms of prayer either in the storefront setting or in the homes of the people. These servant forms of ecumenical services have been recommended decades ago, as reviewed in the New Delhi Report of 1961 in the

Section on the Unity, Third Assembly of the World Council of Churches: "Implications of Local Church Life" 20 (a) by W. Vister Hooft, ed.,: London:

> There is need for an increase in opportunities of growing together as local churches: Through common worship, Bible study groups, prayer cells, joint visitation, and common witness in our communities. Locally as in the whole ecumenical movement, we should be especially ready in Christian love to seek out and to establish fellowship with those traditions and minorities to which we are not now related. Even where we are compelled to remain separate at present in central aspects of the life of our congregations, there is considerable freedom for developing areas of common worship, witness and service in homes and communities. (The Unity of the Church, p. 90).

The Ecumenical Parish. In areas of concentrated interfaith activity where religious, educational, social or political concerns are shared, such as in university, medical or legislative centers, the ecumenical parish could proclaim a needed missionary sign of ecumenism to all churches and religious bodies. With the increasing possibility of an ecumenical solution to the problems of intercommunion, as recently witnessed with Pope Francis and Orthodox Patriarch Bartholomew in Jerusalem (May 25, 2014), this kind of parish could be constituted as a Eucharistic community through which families of interdenominational marriages could jointly practice a common Christian ecumenical faith. It is significant to remember that the Greek word "orthodoxy" signified the same meaning as the Latin word "catholic" before the Reformation which truly Patriarch Bartholomew and Pope Francis were *interactively witnessing* and *liturgically celebrating.* With such a sacramental binding of this *intercommunal* image, this innovative parish could fulfill a more consistent ecumenical role in a pluralistic society through common worship and joint involvement in Christian social action.

The ecumenical parish could also be productive of more efficacious pastoral planning with which ministers and priests in educational and hospital chaplaincies could share common official ministries. It could, for example, provide new possibilities for collegial campus assignments and collective hospital ministries designed to serve academic studies and sick people in a more communal context than is possible through traditional organizational chaplaincies. Within college and university chaplaincy assignments, traditional and structural denominational climates limit the missionary endeavors of chaplains so evident in the contemporary sexual scandals of fraternities' and sororities' subcultural activities. The ministerial chaplaincy structures on university and college campuses have been traditionally structured by parochial and denominational subcultures. Opening the symbolic interactional boundaries of ecclesiastical chaplaincies toward ecumenical religious ministries could more efficaciously engage *leadership, building* and *reconciliatory* missionary programming among infrastructural faculty and student bodies toward changing the sexual mores of collegial structural functional dormitories and within the interpersonal anxieties of fraternities and sororities. Moreover, the ecumenical parish could also provide a desperately needed change in the chaplaincies of military assignments whose chaplains are sometimes restricted by traditional bureaucratic medical and psychiatric regulations of government channels and ecclesiastical structures from exercising the prophetic and counseling offices of their ministries.

These innovative forms of ecumenical communities would vary according to the degree of fellowship and the intensity of commitment among the membership. It would also be dependent on the permanent or temporary association that the members might have with a specific community itself or with the particular institution to which the community might be attached. More often than not, however, a plurality of forms, as described in these proposed models, could be serviceable in one given area and could co-exist with a more traditionally structured residential parish. In this latter setting, the bishop could invite his Protestant and Orthodox episcopal colleagues or the corresponding proper authorities to appoint a minister and priest to assume the co-responsibilities of official ministry with his appointed priest. By extending the principles of collegiality and reciprocity to embrace other offices of authority and other forms of ministry, such a gesture would indeed open new ecumenical directions in the common quest for Christian unity.

Professional or Occupational Communities. Certain associations of profession or occupation which bring together related groups of Christians in a stable, quasi-stable or even transient manner could offer a truly responsive sign of Christian life and ethics to the social, economic and cultural orders with the establishment of parish communities structurally adapted to the work of the profession or occupation. Professional or occupational communities could be formed accordingly for such groups as doctors, lawyers, public officials, merchants, workers, actors, etc., to enable them to experience the sustaining support of a Eucharistic Gospel fellowship in the face of increasing stress from the complex social and ethical issues of their work. Communities of this type could supply profound resources for their members in their professional or occupational moral dilemmas and could assist them to make a significant missionary impact on society as well as on their particular profession or occupation.

As an example of such communities, a kerygmatic form of Christian actors and actresses could be developed with a repertory theater company. Through the medium of religious and secular drama, the theater troupe traveling and performing as a community of artists dedicated to Gospel values could reach appreciable numbers and influential segments of the silent majority. With such a prophetic purpose, the community could be set up in any given resort area to perform a series of plays composed to speak out on the social and ethical implications of current issues. Through the contacts of interested tourists, the community could arrange for off-season tours to various local areas throughout the country. Because of the inter-diocesan and ecumenical nature of such missions, the communities could be co-sponsored by the National Conference of Catholic Bishops and the National Council of Churches, whose services could be ecumenically utilized for any necessary spiritual or pastoral direction of the work.

Living perhaps in the form of the semi-monastic commune, the community itself would be a sign of faith and hope to the contemporary theatrical world, so many of whose artists perform amid personal and professional struggles against faith and hope. It would, at the same time, be a sign of love and acceptance of other playwrights and actors who, through the media of the arts, are also responding to God's mission in secular domains.[11]

> Literature and the Arts are also, *in their own way,* of great importance to the life of the Church. For they strive to probe the unique nature of man, his problems, and his experiences as he struggles to know and perfect both himself and the world. They are preoccupied with revealing man's place in history and in the world, with illustrating his miseries and joys, his needs and strengths, and with foreshadowing a better life for him. Thus they are able to elevate human life as it is expressed in manifold forms, depending on time and place....Efforts must therefore be made so that those who practice these arts can feel that the Church gives recognition to them in their activities, and so that, enjoying an orderly freedom, they can establish smoother relations with the Christian community. Let the Church also acknowledge new forms of art which are adapted to our age and are in keeping with the characteristics of various nations and regions. (Harmony between Culture and Christian Formation, Documents of Vatican II).

"In their own way," the Eternal Word Television Network (EWTN), expresses art forms of ministry, "adapted to our age and...in keeping with the characteristics of various nations and regions." Their upgraded extensive Christological and ecumenical programing has recently projected beyond religious and ecclesiastical productions encompassing international and global coverage of Pope Francis' ecumenical ministries and even producing their own ecumenical projection of newsworthy contemporary global events with daily prime time "News Nightly" broadcasting of political, cultural and ethical commentaries.

Role of the Priest in Structural Adaptation. Inasmuch as the new priest is called to the leadership of a Christian community, the casting of his role in these adapted forms of parish would involve the necessity of acknowledging the specific *role distinctions of leadership* in the personal and communal ministry of the faithful and the public and pastoral ministry of the priest. These distinctions would allow the faithful to resume their privileged place in the ministry by utilizing and coordinating their personal charisms in communal mission for the common good of the Church. They could thus undertake the *charismatic leadership* of the community and would assume the responsibilities of determining its missionary strategy as well as providing for its temporalities. This leadership could be entrusted to an elected board of directors who could fulfill these responsibilities through committee assignments. These distinctions would also allow the priest to assume his proper role of pastoral leadership in the community through the fulfillment of public functions of his cultic, prophetic and ministering offices. By his cultic office, he could unite the community in the Eucharistic body of Christ and to the Universal Church (1 Cor. 10:16ff.) and would reconcile the members in their internal disputes as well as in any external estrangement from the unity of God's people that they may suffer in wandering from the truth. *By his prophetic office,* he would proclaim this truth through the preaching of the word and would direct the community by this word that its public image may always conform to its biblical image. *By his ministering office,* he could provide for this spiritual care of the community, counseling its members, consoling the disturbed, comforting the sick and through a variety of other services, such as his own prayer, suffering and "ordinary work."[12] In this pastoral capacity, the priest would bear the ultimate responsibility of leadership in the community, inasmuch as by this threefold apostolic office, he could be commissioned by the bishop to oversee the preservation and development of biblical tradition in the community and the building up of its body in Christ.[13] The delicate balance between the charismatic leadership of the faithful and the pastoral leadership of the priest would be maintained by mutual respect for the particular charisms and offices of their interrelated ministries and by the common charism of love in their ministering service. "It is only in the objective exercise of ministering love, of which not only wide knowledge but also discrimination and tact are essential components, that charismatic gifts can be safeguarded against abuse."[14]

The multiple forms of parish community developing from structural adaptation would often demand a plurality of ministerial roles from the priest enlisting not only the services of his pastoral office but his personal charismatic gifts as well. These roles could be filled through several appointments on a full or part-time basis determined by the particular form of the community and the personal charisms of the individual priest. Such innovative manifold roles would maximize the priest's missionary relationship to the external environment and would extend his ministry into areas of the secular, hitherto untouched by the traditional style of the parish priesthood. So, expanding the pastoral boundaries for the priest, these roles would enable him to serve the widely diverse needs of people living and working in pluralistic social orders. The ecumenical diversities of these roles would, moreover, provide him with abundant opportunities to make the "new adjustments" in contemporary global ministries required by Vatican II for a changing church in a mobilized globe at the cosmological edge of an apocalyptic world, where ISIS needs CHRISTIS!

Evaluation: Structural Adaptation and the Underground. There is no doubt that in some sections of the church these kinds of adaptation to traditional parish structures would be met with some degree of opposition. In many instances, the strength of such widely accepted intra-organizational movements, as in ecumenism and in liturgy, could provide the necessary resources for implementing these changes. In other instances, however, it might be imperative for the priest, so convinced of the urgency for adaptation, to take the community underground. In the event that this strategy would be required, it should be remembered that this extra-organizational adaptation could be an enriching experience for the whole church inasmuch as the priest and people, committed to this radical stance for church reform, would paradoxically manifest a new sense of loyalty to the church precisely for courageously acting as catalysts for change in spite of the personal and professional risks involved. The terrifying ISIS martyrdom of Kayla Mueller's death gives testimony of her interpersonal apocalyptic faith (see USA TODAY, February 24, 2015).

It would be important in such cases to open the fullness of the priest's historical perspective that he might view the temporary record of "disobedience" in the light of true tradition and in the vision of responsible faith. It should be stressed that so electing this course of church reform for higher motives than blind obedience (for which there is ample precedence in the New Testament and in church history) would not only be responding to the needs of numbers hoping for more liberating ways to celebrate their faith but would often help him to realize a new sense of freedom in his own work. This position could enable him to explore new roles of ministry in less clericalized forms. By force of sheer monetary imperatives, he would have to seek a secular occupation requiring a different ministerial lifestyle and a more common place of residence. In a progress report of its study on the life and ministry of the priest, the theology subcommittee appointed by the National Conference of Catholic Bishops acknowledged the need for such changes:

> "Clerical culture" refers to a sociological texture woven of distinctions and privileges which set priests apart from American society. Its multiple strands are constituted by the dependence on rectory living, clerical garb, titles, isolated seminary education, exemption from military service, preferential treatment, and most of all, by celibacy. Those priests who value such a lifestyle should be free to pursue it as they see fit, but those who do no should be equally free to relinquish it. Priests gratefully acknowledge that many of these privileges have been accorded them by a generous and well-meaning laity, but the priests' deep concern for that same laity prompts them to put aside a distinctive "clerical culture" in order to serve others more effectively.[15]

These changed conditions for ministry would be more consistent not only with the present socio-economic patterns of life and work but also with possible future psycho-social patterns of multiple professional commitments.[16] Hence, in addition to increasing the possibilities for the priest to extend his ministry through a plurality of organizational relationships, the benefits that could accrue from this exploratory adaption in different ministerial lifestyles would hasten the day for the de-clericalization of the ministry and the de-bureaucratization of the church.[17]

MODELS OF GOAL SUBSTITUTION

By substituting other goals that are more secular in nature and more universal in need than traditional parochial goals, the following set of models would enable the church to respond more efficiently in contemporary Christian mission to urgent situations inadequately served by traditional parochial forms. In this way, these models could open the church to new experiences of parish through the dynamics of a movement. According to Gregory Baum, a movement is defined "by its mission or function in the wider community to which it belongs." He insists that "the sociological model for understanding the Christian church today is 'the outer-oriented movement.' "[18] He further states that "the church as movement would intensify the people's involvement in the life of society. Through conversation and common action, the church would draw men more deeply into the mystery of redemption present in human life."[19] As such, the communities presented in these models would frequently involve the borrowing of certain ideologies like those of the Peace Movement, the Civil Rights Movement or the Anti-Poverty Movement and theologically endorsing them with a faith commitment that would entail an intensified involvement in social action through a self-sacrificing gospel service to humanity. The structural form of these movements in terms of Christian community would vary widely depending on the nature of the substituted goals and the kind of ideological or political organization in concern. For example, communities, collectives or communes could be formed in a given location by those engaged in community organization work, the peace movement or the youth movement.

The VISTA Collective. The whole concept of AmeriCorps VISTA could have been conceived from the pages of the New Testament. It represents a true and contemporary expression of secular mission. However, volunteers who would prefer a close structural identification with a form of Christian communal mission in the secular could group together in a collective within which they could live or at least share together some material goods, such as food, an automobile or motorcycle and other utilities. They could invite people with whom they work and for whom they serve to participate in the collective in relative degrees depending on the frequency of their association and the intensity of their commitment. The members could occasionally worship together in their homes or in other suitable places of their work and express a common witness through careful and relevant strategies for Christian social action. Such an approach to this secular mission would indeed strengthen the ties among the workers and could even instill in them a deeper and stronger commitment to the voluntary service.

The Shalom Community. A great missionary service to violent America could be rendered by Christians united in community through faith in quest for national and international peace. Committed to a just, political and social reform through non-violence and sustained by the spiritual support of communion through Eucharistic services and common interaction, these peacemakers could express a more effective sign of peace by organized communal witness than by the often isolated efforts of individual conscientious objectors. In this respect, the supportive bonds of community would be immeasurably sustaining to certain members who might feel called to risk imprisonment or other punitive sanctions for necessary, conscientious violations of civil law. Moreover, as the community would share many common interests with more militant groups and would seek their many related goals, it could conceivably influence some revolutionaries, through exemplary strategy and action, if not through dialogue, to select more appropriate peaceful means for revolution which more faithfully conform to the principles of Christian social ethics.

The Sanctuary. The highly successful rehabilitative efforts for drug addicts by those involved in youth work or in counter-cultural movements could draw the church more deeply into the mystery of redemption present in human life. This work, basically counseling in nature, would intensify the Christian's involvement in the life of society, were the church willing to form therapeutic communities for drug addicts and for those engaged in drug work. Respecting the alternative modes of therapy for drug prevention and treatment, various communities could be established to serve the diverse needs of those addicted to drug use. The Sanctuary, for example, could take the form of a crisis intervention center where those who may be "tripping" could find communal comfort, sensitive care and supportive reassurance. With the staff forming the nucleus of a Christian community, provisions could be made for occasional common worship and for open group discussions on the religious aspects and transcendental explorations of para-liturgical arts associated with musical and ballet performances (see Guerrette Volume II, 2015, p. 37). The Sanctuary could thus offer some enduring spiritual motivation to drug abusers along with its therapeutic hospitality. This approach to drug work could attract the addict to return to the Sanctuary regularly by enlisting from abusers a commitment to the service of other addicts in need of their help. Such a fresh experience of their sense of personal dignity and value in relation to their membership and service in and through the community could provide the necessary crutch for continuity in the rehabilitative process of their permanent cure and health.

Role of the Priest in Goal Substitution. The role of the priest in these forms of Christian community would generally revolve around the prophetic office of evangelical ministry. By his response to lead the particular movement in the proclamation of the gospel message to the wider community, the priest would often have to *substitute* the biblical role of the prophet to remind politicians of their duties to change the system to meet the needs of the people and the nation. Ever conscious of the admonitions of the Jesus the Prophet, who changed the system of the Sabbath to meet the needs of the people. (Mk. 2:27–28), he would frequently be called to express his commitment in an exemplary manner of self-sacrificing service to reverse the sinful, social or political conditions confronted (Mt. 23:13–39). At times, heroic witness might be required of him, as has been the case with Father Groppi and the Berrigans (Phil. 1:12–14); but, more often than not, his prophetic office would be utilized for the purpose of leading the members of the community in reconciling the wider community and its political leaders to the New Testament goals for justice and rights and for peace and love. The cultic and ministering functions of the priest's office would be fulfilled in accordance with the particular communal form that the movement would take. His role of leading the community would, in general, be expressed according to the distinctions made above regarding charismatic and pastoral leadership.

Evaluations: Goal Substitution and Politicization. Inasmuch as these movements are usually related to networks of national organizations and, as such, are independent from the church regarding their nature and purpose, their existence and their mission in Christian community would, in large measure, be self-determined. These various situational factors could, as a matter of course, present some problems for the official church in terms of ideological politicization and hierarchical conflict. Substituted goals could, at times, be contrary to the normally accepted policies of the ecclesiastical authorities. These difficulties, notwithstanding, could be resolved in most cases by a specialized and tactful priest who could not only provide the spiritual insight to properly relate the ideology of the substituted goals with the theology of missionary goals but who could also guide the members of these movements to assume personal, communal and ecclesial responsibility for their activity vis-à-vis the ultimate accountability of the bishops.[20]

MODELS FOR RESPECTING LATENT RELIGIOUS VALUES

With the changes introduced into the church through the adaptation of its structures and the expansion of its goals, the following models of Christian community would represent the most important forms for its organizational re-creativity. Designed to respect the latent religious values of more conservative Christians, these models would preserve the basic form of the territorial parish and stabilize the traditional role of the parish priest. The preservation of latent values and the stabilizing respect of the ministerial pastoral role, however, would not anchor the people and the priest to the past; but could provide for them, in the associative grounds of these other innovative models, exploratory options toward their response to the rapid pace of social and religious change.

Local Parishes. Since not all Christians are endowed with the same charisms and hence not called to the intense degree of missionary involvement, local congregations would still represent the ordinary form of parish. Respecting the natural groupings of people in given areas, local parishes could furnish genuine expressions of close worshiping communities oriented toward the universal community of all men. Accessible to every ethnic, racial, occupational, professional, and age group in this historically latent form, these parishes *could be* meaningful signs of the catholicity of the church with incentive aids to project attitudes to universal realities. Through more serviceable structures of diocesan, regional and parish councils, they could open the needed channels of inter-parochial communication and collaboration in the apostolate, thus avoiding the narrow enclosures of parochialism. Opportunities for such incentive-building memberships in these local parishes would be determined by the preservation of efficient communication, especially in worship and in witness, and through the interpersonal bonds of lay apostolate incentives for ministerial pastoral service. Such small parish congregations would be unencumbered by the conservatory weight of institutional holdings, like parochial schools for children and financial burdens for educators, and would be individually staffed by a priest, a deacon, married or single, and two sisters free to do ministerial work, as deaconesses.

Role of the Priest in Respecting Latent Religious Values. Although the role of the priest in the local parish would be somewhat structured along traditional lines, the ministerial goal of forming genuine Christian community, as redefined by the Council[21] on the Ministry and Life of Priests, and as underscored by a reduction of boundaries and administrative duties, would allow for a greater emphasis on his pastoral leadership. With the establishment of a parish council which could assume the full responsibilities for the charismatic leadership of the parish, as suggested above, the priest would be in a more favorable position to concentrate on developing *active* pastoral leadership in the community. With the assistance of the deacon and the sisters and the cooperation of appropriate committees of the parish council, he could devote full time to creating gospel fellowship in the parish. Close to the people through his ministering visits, he could sustain them in the insecurity of their confusion over changing religious values and of their fear of changing pastoral forms. By so "tending" the "management" of his ministry in the conventional role expected by his parishioners, he would be an interpersonal help to them in re-building their thrust and a supportive sign for them toward preserving their latent religious values. By so "maintaining" the traditional parochial "patterns" of this more liberal ministerial style, he would, moreover, provide the necessary framework for their identification in familiar congregational forms. In the meanwhile, his exposure to current developments in theology, through a continuing professional education center[22] and to local developments in pastoral reform through the diocesan and regional councils, would hopefully incite him to more actively prepare his parishioners for the values of church renewal.

Evaluation: Latent Religious Values and Transition. During this period of transition, it would be crucial that the latent religious values of more conservative parishioners and older priests be respected in the pastoral processes of transitional change. By conserving the basic form of the congregation, the local parish would not only permit such people to find sufficient coherence for self-identity in coping with the socio-religious problems of church reform, but it would also provide the proper setting through which their exposure to developing religious values and changing pastoral forms could be redeeming. Through the retention of his role as pastor, the older priest would continue to find a customary work climate which would be so necessary for continuity in his work performance as well as in the preservation of his self-image and role in the ministry. Older parishioners would likewise continue to find a comfortable parish climate in their "protective" congregations which would be so necessary for continuity in the preservation of their faith values and their hope through their waning years. However, by so re-ordering its ecclesial priorities at the expense of its institutional and economic values, the local parish could be redeemed of its structural pathological attachments to the past. Moreover, by so reassessing its latent religious values, the local parish could inspire its congregation to redevelop its parochial structures into *more communal forms* through which its priest and parishioners could experience together the integrity of *collaborative* Christian ministry in their respective official and charismatic roles. In such a therapeutic organizational climate where the rich soil of conservative tradition could be re-cultivated by the seasoned gardeners of the faithful, newer forms of pastoral life could grow into younger lay ministerial offshoots for contemporary mission. In a church so protected by these *latency models* in whose congregations, dormancy would be metamorphic rather than paralytic, no parishioner would be prone to experience pastoral disintegration.

Chapter 4
MODELS OF INTEGRATION

As the keystone to organizational unity, the following set of models completes the archway upon which the continuing work of pastoral reform would be constructed. Supportive to the structural components of all the other forms of Christian community, these models would consolidate the membership of the local diocesan church and conjoin its ministerial work. They would constitute the structures through which bishops, priests and people could efficiently collaborate in their common missionary task of building up the *ecclesial* Body of Christ.

The Sectional Parish. Respecting the sociology of community in its pluridimensional forms of the family unit, the neighborhood group, the congregation, and the general community, the larger traditional mother parish could more readily create Christian fellowship by individually sectionalizing into smaller communities at the level of the neighborhood group. Each section could be assigned to a priest or deacon who would act as pastor of the community and would be totally responsible for its pastoral care. During the week, intense concentration could be given to the development of communal spirit and action within the section through liturgical and pastoral programs in homes and neighborhood centers. Informal gatherings for home Masses and discussions could be organized on a regular schedule at these locations, drawing the family into the communal bonds of the neighborhood. On Sundays, the priests and people of each section would assemble at the congregational level in the parish church to observe the Lord's Day without distinction of their respective sections, thus manifesting a visible sign of the unity of the whole worshiping community.

The administrative work and charismatic leadership of the sectional parish would be entrusted to a sectional council whose elected representative would in turn serve on the larger parish council. Delegates from this council would comprise the membership of the regional and diocesan councils. The purpose of these multiple level councils would be to coordinate the work and mission of all the neighborhood sections and to promote the unity of the congregational parishes within the diocese.

Finally, and by way of an example of a unified diocese collaborating in the work of the apostolate as a *symbolic servant church,* an inter-diocesan network of co-operative parish missions could be established within the interactional framework of the multiple level councils.[23] Through this network, the neighborhood section and the congregational parish could then project their common concerns and efforts into other deprived sectors of the larger diocesan and secular communities.[24] These interconnecting ties would strengthen the ecclesiology of the neighborhood and the congregation since the residential character of these sub-divisional levels of community not only insulates suburbanite Christians from the concentrated areas of need in which they are called to *serve* but actually identifies urban Christians in such segregated areas of need from which they are called to emerge.[25] In this context, the designation of a particular urban ghetto as a sectional parish with a part-time priest or deacon would indeed help to awaken its inhabitants with hope to remove the "stone" away from their "tomb."

The Team Parish. In larger parishes unable to be sectionalized, Christian fellowship could still be achieved through a team approach to ministry which would incorporate the services of priests as co-pastors, deacons as assistants, and sisters and the faithful as mission workers. As a balanced expression of official and charismatic ministries in a more traditional setting, the teamwork would include programming for the social apostolate as well as for domestic and congregational liturgies. These programs would be coordinated in the regular sessions of the parish councils composed of the ministerial team and of adequate representation from different age levels in the parish. They would be planned to respect the pluralistic dimensional forms of community mentioned above and would be implemented according to the distinct ministerial roles of the team. These efforts could be facilitated especially through the council's participation in the diocesan and regional network of its team parishes.

Role of the Priest in Integration. Insofar as the plan for pastoral reform employed in the integration models has been designed to break down the larger parishes into smaller more manageable sociological units, the priest's prime target in serving these units through his pastoral leadership would be the small family-neighborhood group. At this nuclear stratum of society, he would find the appropriate psycho-social conditions where his hearers could be favorably disposed to hear the gospel message of Christ and to respond with intent.[26] Celebrating the liturgy and sharing the word in this context, he could instill in them a corporate sense of the Christian life and form with them a corporate team for Christian mission.[27] Following up this communication by personal contact with his ministry of pastoral care through home visitation, he would be closely associated with families, with youth and with the poor, the sick and the aged. His role with these people would be to protect them from the introverting traps of loneliness and isolation to the wider ranges of community and universal concerns. Through his particular association in the various councils on which he would serve and through his actual contacts with other families in cooperative parish mission, he could make this projection a realized experience for them in terms of mutual visitation or personalized spiritual interaction.

Another crucial form of priestly service in these kinds of parishes would be the integrative role of reconciling the old and the young. Since it is precisely within the infra-structural confines of the congregation, the neighborhood and the home where the generations clash, the priest would have to be prepared to experience numerous conflicts from the mixture of these diverse groups at each level of the parish. The old would seek him out for reassurance and stability, while the young would look to him for support and identity. He would, in effect, be frequently cast in the role of reaching out to both generations in these complicating times of transition. His outreach, however, would be a constructive and rewarding experience in building up the corporate *pastoral* Body of Christ. Through this role, the priest would help to preserve the solidarity of the community and to promote the missionary efficiency of its members.[28]

Evaluation of Integration: Church Unity and Missionary Efficiency. Inasmuch as the specific purposes of the integration models would be to preserve the unity of the Church in the total range of pastoral reform and to increase the multiplicity of its missionary efficacy, evaluating these models would involve the explanation of just how these objectives would be achieved. Since almost all efforts for structural adaptation and goal substitution would necessarily take place within the geographical areas of the traditional parishes or their sections, priests assigned to these integrative forms would hold the key to organizational unity and cooperative ministry. Rather than regarding the emergences of these new forms as competitive threats to their parishes, they would look upon them as associative enterprises in the *common missionary work of the Church.*[29] With such an attitude of trust and acceptance, they would be in a position to develop an *exemplary consciousness* among their parishioners by encouraging them to regard the members of these innovative communities as committed Christians called to a specialization in the apostolate. By extending the parish facilities to the members of these communities for their mission projects and by promoting dialogue between them and their parishioners, the priest as a "superior coordinator," would also create a congenial climate where collaboration in mission could be achieved.[30] In the event that numbers of their parishioners would feel called to join these communities or to form new ones as a result of this exposure, the priests would then be in a position to reform their parishes in conformity with the smaller latency models where Christian community would be more viable in a less mobilized context.

EVALUATION OF THE PLAN

Integration and Episcopal Leadership. While missionary efficiency would undoubtedly be promoted with the collaboration of the official charismatic ministries of Christians, the integrative efforts to achieve solidarity in the Church within the total range of pastoral reform, as presented by the above sociological plan, would ultimately depend, however, on the support of its episcopal leadership. No longer constituted on the MBO vertical lines of a top-heavy authority base, this leadership would itself enjoy the horizontal collegial support of its members who, through their cooperative MBE ministries, would share in the decision-making responsibilities of ecclesiastical polity in accordance with the theological principle of collegiality. In this kind of hierarchical system, the Bishop would be cast in the role of a *superior coordinator* charged with the administrative responsibilities of integrating the specialized and diversified ministries of the four modal sets into the integrative ministry of Christ. In such an innovative capacity, he would no longer be isolated from priests and people in structured functional authority roles of diocesan chanceries but integrated as an *engaged leader*, supportively involved in their integrative efforts as well. Through the collegial process of leadership, the bishop would be relieved of the burdens of overly centralized responsibility and absolutized accountability. He would thus rescue the polity of the church from the narrow confines of organizational task-performance and authoritarian system-maintenance, sharing through interpersonal collegiality its policy determination with his priests and the faithful. In this way, he would serve to equalize the official and charismatic ministries of the church, charging them both with sharing the responsibilities of adapting structures and expanding goals. Acting as the chief *integrator* of the diocese he would supervise the coordination of these adapted structures and substituted goals with the latent traditional religious values of the church. When, for example, an innovative form of Christian community is born in his diocese, the bishop would father this "organization" *child* in his "ecclesial" *family*, even if it were unwanted by the latency of traditionalist canonical values. He would be actively engaged in caring for its support, especially by communicating its needs to the other members of the diocesan household.

As an episcopal *father*, he would be in a strategic position to create a basic compatibility among the members of this domestic household and could easily interrelate their various ideologies and goals. Inasmuch as this household contains a hierarchical sub-system in collegial ministry, it would be imperative for the bishop to open the lines of communication between this neophyte community and the pastors of the area in which it was born. By preparing these priests and their parishioners for this *familial* structural change, the bishop would set the pace for the interactional process of Parsonian *adaptive* upgrading and would interactively create the paternal and familial harmony for an exemplary consciousness. These harmonious relationships could be most favorably formed were the bishop to visit the new community with several of these pastors offering his cooperation and sealing its trust by personally presiding over some of its liturgies. So inviting the confidence of these innovative pastoral communities and so enlisting the active support of the more traditional parishes, the bishop would initiate the Parsonian *integrative* leadership imperative of utilizing his episcopal office to coordinate its organizational *caring* functions for the purpose of consolidating the work of MBE pastoral reform in his diocese.

In such an integrative setting, the constitution of collegial authority relationships would be sealed and strengthened by the interdependence and specialization of official and charismatic ministerial roles among the hierarchy and the faithful.[31] In the end, the organizational conditions created by this kind of episcopal leadership would not only be productive of an integrative practice of Christian ministry but would, moreover, be promotive of the psychological success and career growth of priests.

While this sociological plan for pastoral reform would offer the church a flexible system for collegial authority relationships in the integrative practice of ministry and more productive organizational conditions for the priest, it would also introduce a desperately needed system for the institutionalization of change in the church and in the ministry.[32] As both the Fichter and the Schallert-Kelley studies revealed, the church and the priest are sociologically and theologically conditioned by the continuity of social and religious change.[33] On this account alone, it is the responsibility of the church to provide an institutionalized system through which the priest can creatively respond to the continuously changing demands of his ministry by making the required role adjustments without renegade sanctions. In such an integral system as represented by the above models, the church would be in a position to handle change much more efficiently and positively. While it might not be able to officially approve every innovative experiment of the underground movement, it would be sufficiently AGIL to maintain at least unofficial communication with its innovators. Through this kind of integrative dialogue, the official church could learn from its continued openness to review the unapproved experimentation while the underground could be encouraged to reassess its position in view of the common good of the universal ecumenical Church.

SUMMARY AND CONCLUSION

Integrative ecclesiology and missionary efficacy. The application of the AGIL scheme of Talcott Parsons to the system problems of the institutional church has suggested a practical sociological plan for its pastoral reform. According to this plan, four sets of models of Christian community have been proposed for a church in a mobilized society with a variety of pastoral alternatives in each set through which priests, together with the faithful, could express a particular style of Christian witness in diversified forms of official and charismatic ministries. Designed to restore the balance among these complementary forms of ministry, these models would promote the development of an *exemplary consciousness* for faith and mission among all Christians, thus fostering ecclesial solidarity and missionary efficacy. By so creating an integrative ecclesiology, these models would also produce a diversity of interdependent and specialized roles in Christian ministry shared harmoniously by the priests and faithful and coordinated collegially by the bishop. As this plan would integrate the differentiated systems and subsystems of the institutional hierarchical church, it would invite the bishop to assume a more engaging episcopal leadership as a *superior MBE coordinator* and to prepare his priests and the faithful to positively encounter the problems of rapid social and religious change. While it would give the church the required "agility" to introduce new processes into its systems through adaptive upgrading, it would respect the evolutionary process of change and would provide for its *ecumenical reformation*. Moreover, building on conciliar directives, this plan would open to priests manifold secular and pluralistic roles for contemporary ministry and would encourage them to make new and necessary adjustments in their professional careers. With these integrative MBE ecclesiological models and their productive organizational forms of interpersonally *caring* ministries, priests could begin to redefine their role in the church, as the *Mystical Body of Jesus Christ*, and could hope to experience their corporate re-identification with Him as the ultimate Eternal High Priest.

NOTES

1. See *Economy and Society*, Free Press, Glencoe, Illinois, 1956, pp. 16–19. The above explanation represents a fundamental exposition of Parsonian theory as it applies to the functional problems of any social system. Parsons later developed this theory to include the process of the ongoing evolutionary change in organizations by illustrating how the transitional stages of systems are related to certain evolutionary universals which constitute the structural foundations of modern society. Inasmuch as his theory is primarily concerned with the internal organizational needs of systems adapting to changing environmental conditions, his work contains some important implications for the adaptive capacity of the institutional church to cope with the process of the ongoing developments in ecumenism as well as for the functional aspects of its mission to a constantly changing society in pluralism. See *Sociological Theory and Modern Society*, Free Press, New York, 1967, pp. 490–520. Further, more recent applied implications of Parsons' AGIL theory are developed in Chapter 7 of Volume I *Management by Ethics: Innovative Discoveries for Corporate Ethical and Market Moral Reform*, pp. 204–205.

2. See *Sociological Theory*, p. 493.

3. See "Pastoral Constitution on the Church in the Modern World," art. 44 in W. Abbott, ed., *The Documents of Vatican II*, pp. 245–247.

4. This use of Parsons' scheme is more consistent with the critique of his theory offered by Gibson Winter in *Elements for a Social Ethic*, Macmillan, New York, 1966, pp. 206–208.

5. See "The State of the Priesthood," in *The National Catholic Reporter*, 8:16 (February 28, 1972) 7–10 and 15–17. See K. Rahner, *Theological Investigations II*, Helican Press, Baltimore, 1963, pp. 217–263, esp. p. 249, no. 5, and James F. Besnahan, "Rahner's Christian Ethics," in America, 123:13 (1970) 351–354. See also John G. Milhaven, *Toward a New Catholic Morality*, Doubleday, Garden City, New York, 1970.

6. See K. Rahner, *Theological Investigations II*, Helican Press, Baltimore, 1963, pp. 217–263, esp. p. 249, no. 5, and James F. Besnahan, "Rahner's Christian Ethics," in America, 123:13 (1970) 351–354. See also John G. Milhaven, *Toward a New Catholic Morality*, Doubleday, Garden City, New York, 1970.

7. The church should not be adverse to multiple parish memberships in a mobilized society. As Christians multiply their associations at different levels of a pluralistic social order, they are often in a position to become involved in various forms and degrees of common witness.

8. It would indeed be a loss as well as a grave repetition of past errors in missiological strategy to dismiss the importance and the necessity of adapting structures and methods to cultures and people. See "Decree on the Missionary Activity of the Church," in W. Abbott, ed., op. cit. Although this decree distinguishes between missionary and pastoral activity (6), current developments in ecclesiology would certainly tend to recognize this distinction merely in terms of strategy. Thus, with due allowances for the further important distinctions between permanent cultural conditions of nations (10) and changing cultural phenomena of generations, the message of the decree is most relevant, namely, that the church must enter into culture to "heal it," to "preserve it" and to "perfect it in Christ" (21).

9. For an objective critical study of the contemporary Pentecostal movement in the Catholic Church, see Kilian McDonnell, "Catholic Pentecostalism," in *Dialog* (Winter, 1970). While this study offers major theological criticism to Catholic Pentecostals, it emphasizes the value of their restoring genuine religious experiences in the church and recommends that "bishops involve prudent priests to be associated with this movement."

10. See "Dogmatic Constitution on the Church," art. 8 in W. Abbott, ed., op. cit.

11. The importance of the church's recognizing other forms of mission than its own cannot be stressed enough in an age of pluralism. Its failure to do so has often alienated large sectors of the artist's community. For a helpful discussion of the church's relationship to the world of the arts and its responsibility to the artist, see "Pastoral Constitution on the Church in the Modern World," art. 62 in *ibid.*, and C. Williams, *op. cit.,* pp. 92–97.

12. This term refers to any auxiliary secular occupation in which the priest may be engaged. See R. Brown, *op. cit.,* p. 29.

13. See H. Kung, *op. cit.,* pp. 436–442 and Reinhold Niebuhr on *Man's Nature and his Communities,* Charles Scribner's, New York, 1965 and also Ernst Kasemann, *Essays on New Testament Themes,* SCM Press, London, 1964, pp. 63–94. Neither Kung nor Kasemann develops the potential role distinctions in leadership between the priest and the faithful, as suggested here. While Kung places strong emphasis, in the context of discussing apostolic succession, on the leadership of the priest in the community through his public office of pastoral ministry, he does acknowledge the need for the church to be "open to other and different possibilities" for apostolic succession and pastoral leadership, "such as existed in the New Testament church" (p. 442). As Kasemann outlines the relationship of charismatic ministries to office in the New Testament church, he shows some of the differences that existed, claiming that in the Corinthian church Paul "set his doctrine of charisma in opposition to the theory of an institutionally guaranteed ecclesiastical office" (p. 84). It would therefore seems that the role distinctions in leadership, as herein presented, give some recognition to the Pauline Corinthian tradition within the present Roman Catholic tradition. Moreover, the different possibilities for new relationships in pastoral leadership contained in these proposals, modeled on the New Testament church, and would seem imperative of the contemporary church is to responsibly reach out to numbers of Christians who *are* serving with charisma in experimental communities *without* the leadership of a priest.

14. E. Kasemann, *ibid.*, p. 77.

15. *The Systematic Theology of the Priesthood* (Progress Report Summary), United States Catholic Conference, Washington, 1971, quoted in *The National Catholic Reporter,* 7:26 (April 30, 1971) 12, no. 7.

16. See Warren G. Bennis, "A Funny Thing Happened on the Way to the Future," in *American Psychologist,* 25:7 (1970) 595–608. In Bennis' forecast of organizational forms and professional relationships, it may not always be possible or even desirable to hold with Brown that "ordinary work" should not be "a primary occupation, perhaps, but…auxiliary" *(op. cit.,* p. 29; see note 12 above). Like the charismatic Christian, the de-clericalized priest would not have to make the distinction between ordinary work and ministerial work. All work would be mission oriented. The only useful distinctions would be acquired from organizational therapy and could be applied, for strategic purposes in ministry, to the work involved in the priest's multiple organizational or other professional commitments. Bennis, for example, draws three

distinct sets of role relationships which will enlist a plurality of commitments to various organizations: "pivotal" (more or less permanent), "relevant" (temporary) and "peripheral." He claims that a person who would be pivotal to one organization could have a variety of relevant and peripheral roles in other organizations (pp. 606–607). With the restoration of the charismatic ministries of the faithful, the specifically distinct responsibilities of the ordained priest in terms of the cultic, prophetic and ministering functions of his pastoral office would be fulfilled in accordance with these multiple organizational role relationships without any categorical allotment of official ministerial work to primary or auxiliary occupations. (See below, pp. 130 and 157–160.)

17. For an ecumenical perspective on some practical problems and possible solutions associated with structural adaptation in the Orthodox, Protestant, Anglican and Roman Catholic traditions, see the replies of Athenagoras Kokkinakis, Hebert Roux, Stephen Neill and Johannes B. Metz to "Does Our Church Need a New Reformation?" in *Post-Ecumenical Christianity*, ed., H. Kling (*Concilium*, vol. 54), Herder and Herder, New York, 1970, pp. 58–91. For an imaginative forecast of some possible future forms of a de-clericalized ministry and a de-bureaucratized church, see Ivan D. Illich, *Celebration of Awareness: A Call for Institutional Revolution*, Doubleday, Garden City, New York, 1970, pp. 69–94.

18. "The New Ecclesiology," in Commonweal, 91:5 (1969) 124.

19. The Credibility of the Church Today, p. 208. Inasmuch as Baum would recommend the outer-oriented movement as the sociological model for pastoral reform, he does not allow sufficient room for other Christians in the church who may not be able to identify with his political ecclesiology.

20. In a hierarchical system where the authority relationships are drawn through the horizontal lines of a collegial order and where policy determination is shared by the membership, the burdens of ultimate hierarchical accountability are considerably lightened. This organizational theory makes for good theological practice since, according to the tenets of religious freedom so forcefully outlined by Vatican II, ultimate accountability in matters religious must also be borne by individuals and communities before God. See "Declaration on Religious Freedom," art. 2 in W. Abbott, ed., *op. cit.*

21. See "Decree on the Ministry and Life of Priests," art. 6 in *ibid.*

22. The continuing education of the priest is an essential requirement for the due fulfillment of his cultic, prophetic and ministering offices in the modern church. Inasmuch as God ever speaks to his people in the present through new developments in theology and scientific progress, the priest's role is to relate the revealed Word of apostolic tradition to these new developments that God's truth may be coherently proclaimed in a contemporary context. Furthermore, as current research in liturgical studies and in the social and behavioral sciences suggests critical and constructive methods for implementing changes in worship, in mission and in pastoral care, the priest has the responsibility of utilizing these resources in celebrating a more communalizing liturgy with the people and in serving them with more personalizing ministry. Due to the technical nature of these studies and the need for competent presentation, it is quite apparent that these incessant role responsibilities of the priest can only be met by a full time professionally directed continuing education center. See "Pastoral Constitution on the Church in the Modern World," art. 62 and "Decree on the Ministry and Life of Priests," art. 19 in *ibid.*

23. This intra-parochial model is grounded in the sociological theories of symbolic interactional building of unified communities, binding believers together in smaller liturgical devotional units celebrating Home Masses in neighborhood groupings, as sensitively caring devout members of the Mystical Body of Christ. See Guerrette's Doctoral Dissertation *Emmanuel Servant Community* (1971) Department of Sociology, University of Connecticut. The small local parishes of the latency models could readily be incorporated into this network; see above, pp. 73–75.

24. The small local parishes of the latency models could readily be incorporated into this network; see above, pp. 73–75.

25. See G. Winter, *The Suburban Captivity of the Churches*, Doubleday, Garden City, New York, 1961, pp. 144–147. The author presents a similar plan for Protestant inner city ministry by sectionalizing areas of the metropolis into "cross-sectional" congregations according to

major accessible transportation routes. His objective is to construct a scheme for an enduring bond between suburban parishes and the inner city as an ecclesial manifestation of "an interdependent community of the metropolis ministering to many different groups out of a common center" (p. 144).

26. For a brief but concise summary of some special skills needed in leading small groups, see Michael Argyle, *The Psychology of Interpersonal Behavior*, Penguin Books, Baltimore, 1967, pp. 96–101, 166–169. For some helpful empirical observations on the psycho-social dynamics of small group leadership and integration, see Robert F. Bales and Philip E. Slater, "Role Differentiation in Small Decision-Making Groups," in *Family, Socialization and Interaction Process*, by Talcott Parsons and Robert F. Bales, Free Press, Glencoe, Illinois, 1955, pp. 259–306. This article also presents an interesting behavioral study on role differentiation in the small group which could be quite useful in determining a ministerial strategy for specific charismatic roles. The reader should also consult the last chapter of this book where Parsons and Bales employ the AGIL model to delineate the psycho-social "system problems" of the individual person, the nuclear family and the small group in the process of socialization and role differentiation. These are the precise problems which the priest would encounter in his role of re-forming this level of society into Christian communities (pp. 353–394).

27. The liturgical dimension of small group work in mission is not always accurately understood or appropriately valued. Its importance lies in the very purpose of the priest's mission to form an "aggregate" Eucharistic community out of a small secular group in building up the body of Christ (Eph., 2:19–22). This social religious distinction is well-defined by Francois Houtart, *Sociology and Pastoral Care*, Franciscan Herald Press, Chicago, 1965, pp. 49–52.

28. It is, of course, correct to observe that the problems of latency to maintain the functional system of the *status quo* hinders the interactional system of transition to attain the integrity of developmental morality and the integrative values of ecumenical ministry. The choice of which pastoral model to utilize in managing the implementation of reform, however, would depend on the sociological conditions of the given area, the attitudes of the particular priest and people involved and the specific purposes of *latency to conserve values* or of *integration to preserve unity*. (See Guerrette, 2015, Vol. I ch. 7, pp. 205–211.)

29. See Harvey Cox, *The Secular City*, Macmillan, New York, 1965, pp. 157–158.

30. For some important insights on how interdependent and specialized organizational roles are related to the administrative and political power of a hierarchical system, see Chandler Morse, "The Functional Imperatives," in *The Social Theories of Talcott Parsons*, ed. Max Black, Prentice-Hall, Englewood Cliffs, New Jersey, 1961, pp. 121, 151–152. In this essay, Morse proposes a slight variation of Parsonian theory for hierarchical systems to include a fifth functional imperative, namely, "superior coordination." This imperative could easily be applied to the hierarchical system of episcopal authority in the church and would be reflective of the bishop's supervisory role in the primitive church as administrative overseer (see R. Brown, *op. cit.*, pp. 37–38, 67–68). Such a biblical-organizational image of episcopal authority personalized in the role of a *superior coordinator* would indeed help to tie the bonds of its collegial expression and to decentralize the force of its political power.

31. On the importance of institutionalizing change in societal structures, see Amitai Etzioni, *The Active Society*, Free Press, New York, 1968, pp. 14–15; and especially in church structures, see F. Houtart, *The Eleventh Hour, Explosion of a Church*, Sheed and Ward, New York, 1968, pp. 186–188.

32. Fichter, *op. cit.*, pp. 201–202; Schallert-Kelley, *op. cit.*, pp. 177–178.

33. The kind of dialogue needed to integrate the diversity of innovative pastoral forms in an Ecumenical Church is that exchange of openness in the pursuit of truth which inspires people to appreciate other forms and traditions. See Peter L. Berger, *A Rumor of Angels*, Doubleday, Garden City, New York, 1969, pp. 107–117.

Chapter Five

Innovative Projections toward Ecumenical Ministries

No more charismatic leader in the modern history of the Church has appeared in these centuries than the innovative Jesuit priest, Archbishop and Cardinal—Pope Francis! With such a surprising and projective event, clearly evolving in half of a century after the ecumenical and charismatic *leadership* priesthood of Jesuit priest, Teilhard de Chardin (see Vol. 2), this Pope has *ecumenically* projected the modern Papacy of the Church opening the Vatican cultures of ecclesiastical tradition toward the Parsonian structures of AGIL in terms of structural *adaptation, goal attainment, integration* and *latency* in the Universal Church of God! He has re-creatively and openly *adapted* the structures of the Roman Curia with critical practical (*praxis*) planning, embarrassing the Vatican inner culture of its Cardinals and Bishops (see Ohlheiser, "The 15 ailments of the Vatican Curia, according to Pope Francis," The Washington Post, December 22, 2014, https://www.washingtonpost.com/) and has projectively *adopted* an innovative ministry with his Papal ecumenical outreach to Orthodox Christianity. He has expanded the *goals* of the Church refocusing the Papacy toward the universal world, traveling around the globe compassionately caring and interpersonally embracing children, the sick and the elderly, along with his *latent* charismatic smiling and integratively consulting with adaptive receptions of leaders, presidents, and royalty expanding his ministerial care for all nations. His compassionately sorrowful kissing of an invalid's leprously-like scalp reflects the outreach of his care for the impoverished. Projecting a *persona* of a living Christological ecumenical Pope, he has opened his leadership toward *reconciling* presidents and dictators, impelling President Obama to heal the political breaches of the United States and the Cuban dictatorship of the Castro government. And finally, opening the prodigal divisive wounds of the

Christian Churches, Judaic Synagogues and Abrahamic religions, with his ecumenically embracing arms, he has drawn the ecclesial draperies of the Patriarchal Bishops of Orthodoxies and the Synagogical curtains of Rabbinic Hierarchies in the symbolic interactional ecumenicity of Vatican Garden ecologies (Perini, 2014).

These papal ecumenical projections should be especially helpful in providing such incentives for the priest since they would acknowledge the basic Parsonian theory on the primary sources of change for institutions and could prepare the organizational church accordingly to continuously develop and *adaptively* perfect its own role expectations regarding the ministry. This *praxis* version of AGIL sociological theory would identify the external cultural influences of pluralism in society and the internal motivational interests of ecumenism in denominations of ecclesiology as the primary sources that are presently motivating the church toward re-directing its mission to the world through a pluralistic ecumenical ministry. Concurrently, if such open projections toward plural forms of ministry are expanded for the priest with the "sociological imagination" of C. Wright Mills (1959) and the "creative ministries" of Henri Nowen (1971), his relentless search for ministerial re-identity would induce his incentives for motivating him to rise above his institutionalized parochial role expectations. To this end, a redefined innovative priesthood in terms of multiple ministerial roles and professional career growth would contain some far-reaching ecclesiological, liturgical, educational and ecumenical role expectations for the future forms of ministry in a pluralistic world and an ecumenical church

MINISTRY AND ECCLESIOLOGY

In order to develop and perfect the role expectations for priests, the ministry of the Christian priesthood must be seen in its global ecumenical ecclesiological context. From this perspective, there is only one universal ministry of Jesus Christ and his Body, the Church:

> There is one Body, one Spirit, just as you were all called into one and the same hope when you were called. There is one Lord, one faith, one baptism, and one God who is Father of all, over all, through all and within all.
>
> Each one of us, however, has been given his own share of grace, given as Christ allotted it.
>
> . . . And to some, his gift was that they should be apostles; to some, prophets; to some, evangelists; to some, pastors and teachers; so that the saints together make a unity in the work of service, building up the body of Christ (Eph. 4:4–7, 11–12).

As such, the ministry does not belong exclusively to any particular group of clerics or charismatics; it belongs to the whole Church. Current ecclesiology underscores this conclusion with a missionary interpretation of the doctrine of biblical election:

> Membership in the Church is a sublime vocation. Men are elected by God to become affiliated with the Christian community so that they might share the task of giving explicit witness to what has happened, what is happening, and what will happen in history. The Christian is the one who must publicly attest to his faith in the Lordship of Christ, that all human life and history make sense because Jesus is Risen. And the Christian community has the unique responsibility of announcing this fact to the world, of committing itself to the task of bringing about the Kingdom of God here and now, and of showing others what it really means to live in Christ.
> ... Membership in the Church confers a responsibility and a mission.[1]

As seen, this mission is granted to individuals in community by the Holy Spirit for public order through hierarchical ministry or for private or communal purpose through charismatic ministry. Heretofore, the clerical appropriation of the ministry by the hierarchy offset the balance of ecclesiology in ministry and succeeded in suppressing the ministries of the faithful, not to mention the activities of the Spirit. By respecting the proper role distinctions of offices and charisms, as opened in this study, the channels for the participation of the faithful in the ministry of the Church will be re-opened and the balanced of ecclesiology re-set.

With such an integral and ecclesial reordering of ministry, the hierarchy and the faithful will hopefully be responding to their specific role expectations for gospel mission in a much more unified fashion through community worship and witness. Bishops and priests will no longer be expected to be set apart from the people but, as their public leaders in the pastorate, will preside over their liturgical celebrations and will coordinate their missionary occupations at different sociological levels of ecclesial communities. Emerging as leaders from the people through biblical and democratic elections,[2] they will reverse themselves of their cultic, prophetic and ministering superiority of standing *above* the people before God as more *interactional* intermediary figures of exemplary holiness. They will rather assume a more theologically accurate role of standing *with* the people as their presidents and coordinators, re-enacting with them, in the Corporate Body of Christ, His one mediating universal ministry. Chosen from among the people Heb, 5:1), they will identify with these people in community, guiding them to participate in various liturgical, educational and *ecumenical phases of this one ministry.*

For a more contemporary expression of the ecclesiology of such an integrative ministry, as demanded by modern civilization, the role distinctions between hierarchy and people will no longer be drawn by clerical barriers at the expense of ministerial unity but by professional ties for the expertise of ministerial efficacy. It must be remembered that the radical meaning of the word "clergy" in Greek signifies "inheritance" (*kleros*)[3] and was commonly used in the New Testament and early patristic writings to denote the inheritance of all the faithful.[4] Thus, in these writings, the words "clergy" and "laity" (*laos*) described the same people,[5] namely, the faithful among whom the "lots" of ministry were apportioned by office (Acts 1:26) and by charism (Eph. 4:7). In the early church, the separating effects of clericalism were actually unknown, since the New Testament ministry was, at that time, declericalized and more consistently expressed as *faith-fully* professionalized. It also must be remembered that the earlier meaning of the English word "professional" was not intended to convey an occupational means of support but a proficient source of competency.[6]

In the contemporary age of professionalization, the ministry will require increasing need for more competence among its pastoral leaders. To this end, the cultic, prophetic and ministering offices of priests will be more competently filled by those exposed to interdisciplinary training in the theological, behavioral and social sciences. What will have to be avoided at all costs, however, in a professional priesthood will be the abuses of professionalism which have as much alienating effect among the people as clericalism. A declericalized ministry itself will, in turn, be a safeguard against these abuses, as this style of priesthood will preserve priests from the exclusivity and inaccessibility of professionalism as well as from the impersonal exploitation of its commercial fees. The very purposes of the declericalized form of ministry will be to make ministers and priests accessible to the people as their gospel servants (LK. 22:25–27) and to disenfranchise them from the ecclesiastical economy of stipends and benefices. In a professionalized society and a pluralized culture, priests will no longer need to be dependent for their support and livelihood on the feudalistic offerings of the people. Through their multiple professional roles, they will extend their ministry into secular cultures with the utilization of their own occupational skills and charismatic gifts and here earning their living on a pivotal, relevant or peripheral basis.[7] An appreciable number of them will serve concurrently as pastoral leaders of several communities, in accordance with the diversification of the particular communities and the specialization of their own ministries, with their psychological success and career growth dependent on eschatological values and organizational merits rather than ecclesiastical dollars.

> Now I exhort the presbyters among you—I your fellow-presbyter and witness of the sufferings of Christ, the partaker also of the glory that is to be revealed in the time to come—tend the flock of God which is among you, governing not under constraint, but willingly, according to God; nor yet for the sake of base

gain, but eagerly; nor yet as lording it over your charges, but becoming from the heart a pattern to the flock. And when the Prince of the shepherds appears, you will receive the unfading crown of glory (1 Peter 5:1–4).

Through such a biblical authenticity in professional ministry, priests themselves will be more interpersonally efficacious signs to people searching for authentic life styles and selfless service. Congenial to this declericalized life style, priests will no longer be expected to remain celibate, so choosing this role only if they are blessed by the Spirit of Love with its charism. Moreover, they will be free to serve in the priesthood, if they are blessed by God with the graces of the marriage state, which, by now, needs no proof, scriptural or otherwise, to establish its biblical compatibility with official ministries.

Ministry and Gender Integrity. Balancing the ecclesiological scales of Christian ministry necessarily includes a consideration of the role of women in the priesthood. One simply cannot hope to restore the integrity of official and charismatic ministries in the church, let alone the balance of their distinct roles, if he or she fails to acknowledge the imbalance of the sexes within the hierarchical scales of official ministry itself. This author, however, is in accord with the firm traditional biblical interpretation of priestly Holy Orders quite significantly stressed by our ecumenical Pope Francis. Simply stressed by biblical scholarship and historical tradition, it is ecumenically significant that Catholic and Orthodox theologies are consistent in the tradition of Holy Orders for men only. Such tradition is clearly not a sexist denominational position in the church nor a gender integrity problem of biblical theology. It is simply consistent with historical tradition that role differentiation and gender equality were not polarized nor politicized inasmuch as the Blessed Mother of Jesus was not at the Last Supper nor was she waiting outside the Cenacle to "do the dishes!" Moreover, she was deemed by Jesus to be present with the Apostle John, whom He beloved, and Mary Magdalen another woman at the sacrifice of the Cross, whom He loved also, when all of His other male priests had fled. Gender integrity was at stake here in spite of priestly abandonment and ministerial dis-integrity.

It will be a happy day for the church when the integrity of its official ministries is insured by the Pauline policy that ". . . there are no more distinctions between Jew and Greek, slave and free, male and female, but all of you are one in Christ Jesus" (Gal. 3:28). That day will come, however, when the clerical policies of gender equalities and sub-divisional ministerial identities are redeemed by the ecclesiological forms of a declericalized priesthood. That day, however, must not be forced by over anxious judges, especially at the level of the Supreme Court of the United States relative to the recent decisions on gender equalities and ministerial identities. The recent legal decisions of this Court (June 27, 2015) on gender relationships and marital partnerships are significantly inadequate to convince religious believers relative to the sacramental efficacy for same sexual union. It is not within the biblical nor theological nor even the religious "Canon Law" expertise of the Supreme Court to judge nor to promulgate laws relative to moral theological transgender relationships and same sex marital union partnerships. The traditional and ecumenical moral works of Charles Curran on sexual ethics and moral theology published by the University of Notre Dame Press, the Georgetown University Press and the Southern Methodist University Press have been far more academically qualified to judge the moral legitimacy of gender integrity and moral sexual activity than the Supreme Court judges and their respective associated lawyers (See Curran, 1978 and 2013 and Farley, 2006). A complimentary and more critically political *praxis* judgement on these morally sensitive personal and religious domains of same sexual relationships had been offered in the year of 2000 by Howard Dean, as Governor of Vermont, with the legal terminology of "Same-Sex Unions." In these unions, it is imperative to distinguish between sexual unions of interpersonally devoted lovers committed to the fidelity of love as a reciprocal state of sanctifying *caring* and not as in amorous slated state of gratifying erotic friendship.

Sister Margaret Farley of Yale Divinity School explains these sexual unions with the following sixth stage morally developed caring reciprocities:

> Commitment, or especially frameworks for commitment, are means, not ends in themselves. But they are means of the affirmation of persons as ends in themselves and the endurance of love that is an end in itself for those who want their relationships to hold. At its best, this is why the Christian community still recognizes commitment at the heart of an ethic for sexual activities and relationships. It prevents the use of sexual partners as mere means (for sustaining one's sexual desire and providing sexual pleasure), and it offers the possibility for the integration of sexuality into the whole of one's loves and one's life. It alone offers the possibility of sexuality as the expression of transcendent embodiment in the highest forms of friendship . . . . (2006, pp. 290)
>
> Understanding homosexuality as an inborn characteristic of some persons has been important to the achievement of tolerance and civil rights. Thus far, science has not found the exact key to this inborn characteristic, but there can be no doubt that for many individuals who identify themselves as homosexual, there is their own clear experience of being attracted to those of the same sex from the time of their earliest memories. The inborn character of being gay would not have to depend on a biological cause; for even if it is the result of social and cultural construction, it may be as "unchosen," as unchangeable, and as basic to one's continuing identity as if it were biological. . . . My own view, as should be clear by now, is that same-sex relationships and activities can be justified according to the same sexual ethic as heterosexual relationships and activities. (idem, pp. 294–5)

Ministry and Democracy. To enhance the development of the role expectations from a biblically balanced ecclesiological ministry and the integrative perfecting of the role relationships between official and charismatic ministries, it is important to consider how the harmonious *democratic function of collegial authority* between the hierarchy and the faithful will be determinative of the active participation of all Christians in the *universal ministry* of Christ. It can assuredly be said at this point that the faithful will positively respond to a model of biblical authority from the hierarchy and will actively assume their role responsibilities in charismatic leadership, as specified above. They will gracefully share in the shaping of magisterial and ministerial policy as well as ecclesiastical polity, as if through a trust.[8] Their prophetic voice will be a communal and charismatic guide for the hierarchies of priests, bishops and even the Pope, especially when it speaks unanimously in local, diocesan, and universal communities. It will, in turn, enable the hierarchy to rediscover the supportive ecclesial sources of divine enlightenment for the fulfillment of its role responsibilities of publicly teaching or pronouncing the needed doctrine for the church and the world on contemporary religious and social issues. Through these communicative lines of collegiality, this apostolic voice will be more attentively heard by the hierarchy, because, under its charismatic influence, it will speak more faithfully of the biblical message from the experiences of human life and will respond more virtuously to the situational sufferings of this life. With such charismatic tones, this evangelical voice will be recognized by the hierarchy and, through its inspirational trust, will be expressive of an electorate in the appointment of bishops and priests to diocesan and local churches. Moreover, it will, at long last, project the free *democratic* speech of the faithful into the educational channels of the church and the ecclesiastical policies of its ecumenical affairs.

Ecumenical Ministry and Public Policy. One of the most important public domains of the American democracy that the ecumenical churches need to project into the public body politics of the nation in this contemporary devastating gun culture period is to calculate the moral development need to reform the Constitutional Second Amendment of the rights to bear arms. No other country in the world allows the personal ownership of guns nor bears the hypocritical records of the innocent lost lives of their citizens, with morally under-development pre-conventional fears for public safety and authentic democracy (see Fareed Zacharia, "Change Your Gun Laws America," *Washington Post*, July, 30, 2015). This Second Amendment is not a Biblical revelation of moral development theology and is not in accord with traditional Judeo, Muslim and Christian morality cultures and certainly not reflexive of post-conventional sixth stage MBE caring democracy. It is an international moral embarrassment in global public policy "profiles of courage" to persist in the pre-conventional moral autonomy of the Second Amendment and an immoral sacrilegious catastrophe of the American Libertarian Constitution. There are no honorable libertarian policies in this irresponsible hostile Amendment which integratively reflect the political cultural ethos of the morally post-conventional Constitution that project the ethical culture of contemporary public policy needs. In morally intensive ecumenical ministry, it is ethically imperative to *re-amend* the Second Amendment in accordance with sixth stage MBE moral development policies toward relieving the MBO fears of pre-conventional moralities.

Ministry and Liturgy. With Christian ministry placed in a more integrated ecclesiological context, the biblical character of the Church as God's priestly people will be more effectively signified and the liturgical roles of its communicants and leaders, more appropriately assigned. Christians will thus characterize the theology of the priesthood of all believers in their diversified communal forms; and, as they manifest a distinctive *way of life* in the world through their specialized roles of missionary witness, they will worship God in accordance with this *way,* freely relating their missionary works to their liturgical acts. The institutionalized role expectations of the priest, as a cultic functionary, will then be opened to all of God's people as a worshiping Eucharistic community, with the proper distribution of liturgical roles determined by personal charism as well as by sacramental office. The development of these liturgical role expectations on the part of the institutional church will be realized only as the restrictive rubrics for rituals are replaced with an *open liturgies* for worship.

Open liturgy, much like the term "open education,"[9] will more authentically represent the worship of a free people and will be celebrated by this people as a living experience in praising God: "And continuing with one accord in the temple and breaking bread in their houses, they took their food with gladness and simplicity of heart, praising God and being in favor with all the people" (Acts 2:46–47). Such *lively* liturgical forms will induce appropriate cultic actions from the people expressive of their individual and communal missionary works (*leitourgia*) and will require a new set of liturgical role expectations from the people themselves as well as from the hierarchy. Through these openly inspirational liturgical forms, the people will reclaim their rightful roles to express themselves in worship not only with voice, as in song, but also through movement, as in dance. The free expression of these liturgical roles will be directed by the bishop or priest who, as president of their particular worshiping community, would incorporate the works of its members into the cultic acts of biblical word and liturgical sacrament. This openness in cultic worship will not mean an irresponsible abandonment of ritual or rubrics by the hierarchy; on the contrary, these para-liturgical forms and roles will be utilized for the precise purposes for which they were originally intended, namely, to serve as guidelines for the proper celebrations and orthodox preservation of apostolic tradition, as reviewed in note 8 above. The guided freedom of these formal liturgies will open into the devotional lives of the people and will foster a continuation of the celebration of life in the world through informal communal and familial liturgies and through non-liturgical observances and happenings coordinated with and expressive of their particular ministerial roles as Christians and will promote an openly abundant biblical-liturgical devotional life extending into their secular lives. Inasmuch as these projections cast new light upon the ministry and the liturgical roles and devotional lives of priests and people alike, they also point to new directions for ministry and education.

Ministry and Education. When Christian ministry is viewed in the light of an ecclesiology of Biblical election and a liturgy of the priesthood of all believers, it becomes immediately clear that some radical projections for Christian education and its ministerial roles are in need for reformational planning. If such a democratic membership in the church confers responsibility and mission, and if members are to celebrate their faith in the Lordship of Jesus Christ as a priestly people, it is imperative that the ministry of education be directly aimed at those capable of a faith commitment for mission. What is sorely needed in the church, then, is a reversal of child-oriented schooling to adult-oriented learning in the context of diverse democratic forms of ecclesial communities. This reversal of role priorities will imply a reordered set of educational role expectations for the ministry of Christian education which, according to the ecclesiological balance of ministry, will engage all of the faithful as well as priests and brothers and sisters of religious orders.

Accordingly, religious education will revolve around the prophetic mission of the church and will involve the direct learning experiences from the pedagogy of pastoral liturgy and from the peer group dynamics of interpersonal ministering in Christian community living.[10] The principal resources for learning, then, will be the people themselves. *First,* through the experiences that they will share in the kind of open liturgy described above, not so unlike the pedagogical worship of the classical catechumenate of the third and fourth centuries, they will embody God's on-going revelation in the their community as they re-enact the mysteries of salvation. Their free participatory celebration of the liturgy will constitute for them a direct personal and communal engagement with the liturgies of the Word and Sacraments, enabling them to identify with the biblical characters more interpersonally and with the liturgical rites more efficaciously. *Secondly,* through the experiences that they will share in the interpersonal ministering of community, they will be afforded immediate opportunities for interrelating what they learn in their worship with what they encounter in their lives. These peer group learning dynamics in Christian communal living will ensure them with a kind of reinforcement process not only for deepening their grasp of the truth but for increasing their commitment to love. It is with depth of Christian commitment that inspires the laity and especially the youth of the church to respond to the educational mission and the missionary apostolate by volunteering their faith commitment among the innovative educational models of interactional teaching in the third world with pedagogies for the oppressed (Freire, 1970).

These alternative liturgical and communal forms will constitute the setting for what might be called *open education* in the church and will provide the structures in which the improvement of human life can be experienced.[11] As adult Christians begin to integrate their own human development with their spiritual life, they will more clearly recognize their faith commitment in terms of a mission to *develop human life* in the world. This need for ecumenical ministry is clearly wide open to our cosmological world through the multiple spheres of the technological educational sciences. Notice the latest innovative discoveries of the earth sciences which are exclusively focused by MBO values in terms of the altars of technology. (See Zacharia's Moonshots for the 21st Century, CNN 2/15/15). While these "open education" endeavors are truly incredible scientific discoveries for mankind, they are unilaterally closed to any opening multidisciplinary learning tracks for innovative discoveries toward the philosophical sciences of ontology and cosmology, let alone to the theological windows of spirituality and the ontological discoveries of eternity. What an open education opportunity for the universal religions to explore the MBE windows of ecology through the ecumenical ministries of the Churches, Synagogues and Mosques.

Notice also the more down to earth structures for *open education in ministries* which are especially and practically needed for the youth of the church in schools, colleges and universities. *First,* in schools among the young, an efficacious track toward inducing the learning incentives for children and teens would be to challenge their motivating interests in ecological ministries for the salvation of the planet. An engaging open educational MBE reference for attracting children to ecology studies appears in Volume 2 referring to the "wholly" innocent *Giving Tree* [12] and to multiple ecological descriptions of the rapacious industries of the forest industrial complex and the morally un-developed MBO corporate culture priorities of profit maximization greed.

Second, in higher education schools, such as at Dartmouth College and Penn State University, a much more gravely open education ministerial need is in and among the serious sub-cultural *morally under-developed* higher education need for MBE sexual education in the complex organizational environments of colleges and universities around the nation. These types of counter-cultural sororities and athletic fraternities are prone to rituals of pre-conventional morality and moral under-development fragility, virtually causing grave fears of "psycho-historical dislocation" from the "boundaries" of traditional family identity values and the loss of personal morality and psychological integrity (Lifton, 1969).[13]

Ecumenical education for pre-adults, as a way of looking at the world in view of a specifically *human* response, will be offered through their childhood and adolescent years in the surroundings of Christian community according to a developmental schedule based on the individual's own intellectual and psychological "readiness for religion" (see note 16 below). The ultimate purpose of this ecumenical education for pre-adults will thus be to enable them to grow through these communal structures toward a gradual awareness of the specific difference between a human response to a way of looking at the world and a Christian response *toward dealing with the world.* Inasmuch as the adult members of the community and, in particular, the parents exemplify this Christian response by their "way of life," adolescents will, in their own time, more readily recognize the full implications of church membership in terms of a faith commitment for mission. Their religious education will, in effect, prepare them for the radical choice of converting their human response to life into a Christian response. In the grace of this conversion, they will open their way of life into the *way of Christ* to be set apart with His *priestly people.*

Drawing these projections for religious education from the ecclesiology of biblical election and from the liturgy of the *"priesthood of all believers"* illustrates that the ministerial roles of education in the church belong to the whole Christian community and not exclusively to priests and religious:

> The idea of the priesthood of all believers gradually came to be almost forgotten by the faithful and by most theologians. As a comment on this development, . . . two observations may be made which sum up the whole issue: The fact that the leaders of the community are called "priests" is unexceptionable precisely because of the priesthood of all believers; but the fact that the leaders of the community *exclusively* are seen as "priests," and become a separate cast, after pagan and Judaic patterns, standing *between* God and men and barring the direct access to God which the whole priestly people should enjoy—this as we have seen is contrary to the New Testament message: Both the message of the *one* mediator and high priest Jesus Christ and that of the priesthood of *all* Christians (Kung, 1967, p. 383).

Accordingly, the particular role expectations for the priest in the ministry of education then can be cooperatively fulfilled through the pedagogical functions of his *cultic, professional and ministerial leadership roles,* efficaciously performed in an open para-liturgical climate and in a collaborative context of an associated ministering Christian community of the laity. Gabriel Moran insists on the communal imperative for such an educational ministry in these terms: "Education ought to be a process in which the whole community educates that whole community for the whole of communal life. . . . Without some form of community experience, no educational venture will be successful and an ecumenical education is doubly handicapped."[14]

With such *interactional forms of community* so projected for church renewal through pastoral reform, the ministerial roles of Christian education will be expressed as a progressive learning experience in community opening all the faithful to a triply blessed venture in ecumenism.

MINISTRY AND ECUMENISM

The ministerial venture in ecumenism is indeed blessed with the threefold mission in the areas of Christian ecumenism, religious ecumenism and secular ecumenism. This mission has been described by the late Richard McBrien as a service of pluralism through dialogue by means of which Christians open themselves to encounter with one another, with believers of other religious traditions and even with those who are religiously indifferent. Identifying pluralism as "a value to be promoted and sustained," McBrien stressed the importance of dialogue among its components for keeping it "open-ended" and "living."[15] Projections for this kind of mission to pluralism and for the expectations of its ministerial roles, then, can best be made by outlining a multi-focal vision for ecumenical ministry in terms of an *open ecumenism* which will generate dialogue within and among the three specific areas of *Christian, religious* and *cultural ecumenism*.

Open ecumenism. Before making these pluralistic projections toward an ecumenical ministry, however, it is first necessary to comment on the *role of dialogue* as a means to open the ecumenical movement to a wider projective pluralism. Dialogue in ecumenism has all too often become weary with theological discussions on doctrinal unity and ecclesiastical polity. It can, however, be "the life blood of pluralism," as McBrien would claim, and project ecumenism to open horizons for exploring truth, as John Dunne would claim. Although the latter does not employ the terms "ecumenism" or "dialogue," he nevertheless maps out an exploratory journey for open ecumenism along the paths of a dialogical process of ". . . passing over from one culture to another, from one way of life to another, from one religious to another" and ". . . coming back with new insight to one's own culture, one's own way of life, one's own religion."[16] The most accessory vehicle for this passing over is the disposition of a "sympathetic understanding."[17] Persistently moving toward new horizons on a "voyage of discovery," this disposition constantly *opens* one to new visions into truth through the experiences of "living by insight."[18] While this fascinating and creative use of dialogue promotes the intended unity of ecumenism, it respects the extended diversity of pluralism. Dunne would put it this way: "In the moment of passing over you see your oneness with other men and with God, but in the moment of coming back you see your own concreteness and individuality."[19] In this sense, dialogue is an enlightening ecumenical experience which opens Christians to one another, to believers of other religions, and to peoples of multi-cultural persuasions. Such interactional religious sensitivities project pluralistic ecumenical communities.

Christian ecumenism. Dialogue of this kind will regenerate the spirit of ecumenism among Christians and will bless the church with a strategy for an ecumenical ministry. According to this strategy, new ministerial roles will emerge in the ecumenical movement which will open all Christians to the mission of pluralism and not just to ministers and priests. When Christians begin to understand the dialogue that God initiated with man as a passing over of His Son with sympathetic understanding from eternity into time and from the Old Covenant into a New Testament opening His life toward a Gentile pluralism, they will recognize the ecumenical Spirit of the Father's love and the ecumenical ministry of the Son's mission. They will know how the Son shared His insights with others particularly after He returned to His Father by sending the *Spirit of ecumenism* into His Church, enabling His disciples to continue His ecumenical ministry. Baptized into this discipleship, Christians will freely assume the role responsibilities especially of this ministry guided by Jesus Christ, the exemplar of the ecumenical priesthood. In this way, they will be free to *pass over* into the lives, cultures and religions of other men and to *come back* into their own lives, cultures and traditions of Christianity with enriched insight. So experimenting with truth and with religion, they will share the discovery of their insights with all men, extending the mission of ecumenism to the universal spheres of all religious beliefs and secular concerns. Touched by the *Holy Spirit* of this open ecumenism and moved by its exploratory strategy, Christian ministry will thus be engaged to serve all men with the ecumenical priesthood of the Universal Christ, leading them through the convergence of all religions into the Kingdom of the Father.[20]

Open ecumenism will play an important role within Christianity itself, for it will only be through its spirit and strategy that integration in Christian ministry will be fully attained. In order for the fruitful expression of charismatic ministries to grow in the church, the ecclesiastical climate will have to be such as to foster the *spirit of trust* that comes from a sympathetic understanding and to promote the strategy of dialogue, especially if it comes from *"speaking in tongues"*:

> And when the days of Pentecost were drawing to a close, they were all together in one place. And suddenly there came a sound from heaven, as of a violent wind blowing, and it filled the whole house where they were sitting. And there appeared to them parted tongues as of fire, which settled upon each of them. And they were all filled with the Holy Spirit and began to speak in foreign tongues, even as the Holy Spirit prompted them to speak (Acts 2:1–4).

When Christians open themselves to passing over to other traditions of the church with this spirit and with this strategy, even if they do not experience the miraculous inspirations of "speaking in tongues," they will come back to their own traditions with deeper insights and with "*analogical imagination*" into the ecumenical role expectations for their ministry (Tracy, 1980). In this way, new insights will be discovered, communicated and shared among their respective traditions and will open their vision so that they will know just what kind of unity in faith to confess when they pass over and what kind of diversity in tradition to conserve when they come back. The experiential *flow of passing over and coming back* will help them to enrich their ministry with the spirit of unity and the strategy of dialogue for their creative participation in the continuing process of ecumenism in the future church.

Religious ecumenism. Creative ministry in the future church will require increasing participation in an ecumenical process that opens into the pluralism of other religious traditions. Christians will realize that ministry was not designed by Jesus for the proselytizing purposes of bringing all men into the church but for the missionary purposes of leading all men into the kingdom. They will know that their mission must be prepared to launch into journeys toward this kingdom that will carry them into other religions. They will experience the living God in these different traditions as they recognize the resonance of His Word in unfamiliar scriptures and uncustomary worship. Enriched with new insights into God's revealed truth and into man's common experiences of this truth, they will come back to their own religions ready to share these experiences with others. Without renouncing the creedal and cultic traditions of their own faith on this "voyage of discovery" they will build from the common base that they share with other believers what John Dunne (2011) and Teilhard de Chardin, prior to him, had projected in *The Future of Man* (1964) for this age of ecumenism, namely, a religion of the future through which all men will be led to the Kingdom (see also Dewart, *The Future of Belief,* 1966). For Christians, this ecumenical process will be centered in Christ since they believe that He is "the first-born of all creation," the *Cosmic Redeemer,* in whom all believers will be united (Col. 1:15–20, 27; Eph. 2:11–22, 3:6). Teilhard focused his projection in this way: "A general convergence of religions upon a universal Christ who fundamentally satisfies them all: That seems to me the only possible conversion of the world, and the only form in which a religion of the future can be conceived."[21]

Ecological global ecumenism. This Teilhardian focus on ecumenism is so critically and cosmologically important not only for the "future of belief," but especially for the *future of the planet* (see Vol. 2 on his Christological ecology, pp. 51–54). The recent encyclical on environmental human ecology by Pope Francis engages economists to ponder how "religion can do economics (an ecumenical) favor" toward resolving the multinational political problems paralyzing global market economies of Europe and Greece. What is needed in this MBO international economic crisis is a morally humane virtue of debt forgiveness, as if *"people mattered"* (Schumacher, 2010) and as a liberating grace of sixth stage post-conventional morality:

> This requires the periodic cancellation of debt, recognizing the debts can lead to a form of bondage, like slavery, from which it becomes impossible to escape, producing socially conducing inequality. It is therefore humane and economically sensible to wipe out the slate clean (Simms, 2015).

The ethical rationale for this 6th stage post-conventional MBE morally economic planning has already been proposed by human rights experts of the United Nations specifying the inducement incentives for resolving this international financial crisis. Two United Nations human rights experts, Alfred de Zayas and Virginia Dandan, have critically proposed a moral referendum call for international solidarity:

> All human rights institutions and mechanisms should welcome the Greek referendum as an eloquent expression of the self-determination of the Greek people in conformity with article 1 of the International Covenant on Civil and Political Rights and in pursuance of article 25 ICCPR on public participation. Indeed, a democratic and equitable international order requires participation by all concerned stake-holders in decision-making and respect for due process, which can best be achieved through international solidarity and a human rights approach to the solution of all problems, including financial crises. (United Nations Human Rights, Office of the High Commissioner for Human Rights, Geneva, June 30, 2015.)

Secular cultural ecumenism. Conceiving a religion of the future toward which the ecumenical process is steadily evolving will require the application of the spirit and strategy of open ecumenism to the secular and cultural areas of the ministry to pluralism. Christians will see the *leadership, reconciling* and *building* roles of their mission opening more and more widely into such areas as the social, political, economic and educational sectors of public life and will attempt to serve religiously among different persons or within cultural and political institutions with value insights focused on immediate human and ultimate spiritual goals. *Passing over* into these secular and cultural sectors as individuals, in some instances, and as a community, wherever possible, they will identify with their secular colleagues through common interests and commitments and will share with them their own distinctive eschatological vision. So proclaiming the Kingdom of God in the present to the wider community, they will *come back* to their smaller community more conscious of a worldview and of their own ecclesial self-image as a *sign of hope* in the future to those associated in their respective cultural views.

Accordingly, they will share in a common ecumenical consciousness among themselves and particularly with their fellow Christians of the larger churches, hoping to enrich and to expand their missionary witness to the universal dimensions of pluralism.

When symbolic interactional strategies of ecumenical dialogue are applied in the mission to pluralism within the social structural and institutional areas of Christian, religious and secular ecumenism, there will emerge missionary opportunities for constant interchange of ministerial activity among these three areas. Within these innovative forms of ecumenical ministry, ministers will not be confined to isolated areas of local Christian churches, as constrained by the role expectations of parochialism; they will, on the contrary, be opened through the spirit of ecumenism to the religious and secular areas of the Gospel mission, as demanded by the missionary role expectations of pluralism. Ordained priests, for example, will discover entirely new phases of ministry when it is enriched and expanded to pluralistic missions. As declericalized ministers to a particular Christian community of God's people, they will extend their ministry through the strategy of open ecumenism to the religiously indifferent as well as to those of other religions, sometimes together with the community they serve and other times apart from it. Always enjoying, however, the supportive interaction of the community's fellowship, they will freely move back and forth among the interpersonal bonds of ministerial dexterities. Their pivotal, relevant and peripheral roles of ecumenical ministry will be related to the *leadership, reconciliatory* and *building* functions of the church's cultic, prophetic, and ministering offices. The more successfully these priests integrate the professional roles of their ministries in these three sectors, the more effective will the official functions of their ecumenical priesthood be. So integrating their missionary activities in these three interrelated areas of ecumenism, priests will develop and perfect their Christological ministerial identities and will thus promote their own career growth through multiple professional roles in service of a Gospel mission to pluralistic cultures.

Developing and perfecting one's ministerial identity toward an ecumenical ministry require more than just appropriate incentives and certainly more than just the hypothetical projections that have been drawn from the ecclesiological, liturgical, educational and ecumenical role expectations of a re-defined priesthood. This is a process that calls for continuous multi-disciplinary perspectives of theology and the organizational sciences toward pointing to the need for re-*creatively* institutionalizing ecumenical ministry. However, because of the traditional and historical system problems that would be encountered in all the denominations of the institutional churches toward re-directing their mission to the world, it would be imperative to develop a corresponding sociological plan based on the AGIL model of Talcott Parsons which could draw the structural lines for the future re-identity of Christianity toward a new identity for the re-institutionalized global ecumenical church. In short, an institutional ecumenical ministry would require an institutionalized ecumenical church. Resolving the inter-organizational conflicts of church polity by respecting the inter-organizational functional imperatives of the respective denominations, this sociological plan would not only provide adequate means for the priest to continue the ongoing process of re-identity in an ecumenical ministry but would moreover enable the Christian church to rediscover its ecclesiological unity amid interdenominational diversity.[22] Finally, as the sociological imaginative and historical curtains of C. Wright Mills (1959), briefly opened in Chapter 5 of Volume 1, and now drawn in this "subsequent volume" of *Innovative Discoveries for Ecumenical Ministries*, I pray that these projections of my ecumenical ministries hopefully reflect the *sacerdotal ethos* of the innovative ecumenical ministries of Pope Francis.

SUMMARY AND CONCLUSION

The foregoing set of projections toward an ecumenical ministry have been designed to provide some inducing incentives and subsequent choices for the priest to redevelop and perfect his own ministerial identity. This *praxis* planning has been liberally and critically analyzed to prepare the priest to explore the innovative roles of *leadership, reconciliation* and *building* in the pastoral reformation of the church. New practical symbolic *interactional* identities for the priest have been traced and protectively designed to re-direct contemporary pastoral innovation through the AGIL structural functional theories of Talcott Parsons, as explored in Volume 1 and critically reviewed above in Chapter IV. Acknowledging a need for Parsonian re-constructive planning, from the fundamental sociological theories of Professor Parsons, the external cultural influences of pluralism in society and the internal motivational interests of ecumenism in the church, as the primary sources of change, will direct the priest toward an ecumenical ministry in the pastoral roles of ecclesiology, liturgy, education and ecumenism. While these role-innovative projections for ministry in these areas should help to provide practical incentives for the priest to rise above past and present institutionalized role expectations, their analyses cannot equip him with the means to emerge from these structural parochial roles of the latent past historical denominational parochialism. As critically acknowledged, the above sociological plan for the pastoral reform of the church would indeed induce his *praxis* incentives to make the new adjustments required by manifold roles for re-identity toward an ecumenical ministry in the contemporary church. Meanwhile, it is encouraging to follow the *exemplary ecumenical priesthood* of Pope Francis who has opened his own inspirationally innovative providential search with a "new identity" for the *Pope* toward a "voyage of discovery" exploring the *ecumenical ministry* of Jesus Christ.

NOTES

1. R. McBrien, op. cit., p. 172.
2. See Democratization of the Church, ed. Alois Muller (Concilium, vol. 63), Herder and Herder, New York, 1971, especially Norbert Greinacher, "A Community Free of Rule," pp. 87–107 and Raymund Kottje, "The Selection of Church Officials: Some Historical Facts and Experiences," pp. 117–126. See also note 21 of chapter 4 above.
3. See A Greek-English Lexicon of the New Testament, eds. William F. Arndt and F. Wilbur Gingrich, University of Chicago Press, Chicago, 1957, p. 436.
4. See Acts 26:18; Col. 1:12; 1 Peter 5:3; *The Epistles of Ignatius* to the Eph. 11:2, Rom. 1:2, Tral. 12:3, Phil. 4:1 and *The Martyrdom of Polycarp* 6:2. See also Gerhard Kittel, *Theological Dictionary of the New Testament,* Wm. B. Eerdmans Publishing Co., Grand Rapids, Michigan, 1965, vol. III, pp. 763–764.
5. See Robert Clyde Johnson, "The Christian Ministry, " in *The Church and Its Changing Ministry,* ed. Robert Clyde Johnson, The General Assembly of the United Presbyterian Church in the United States of America, Philadelphia, 1961, p. 26.
6. In the eighteenth century, the word was used to describe one engaged in a learned or skilled profession. It was only later in the nineteenth century that the word came to be associated with one following an occupation as a means of livelihood. The prior usage is, of course, more consistent with an even earlier (fifteenth century) meaning, namely, one committed to a religious profession and with the original Latin meaning, from the root *"profiteri"* one who has made a public profession of faith. See *The Oxford English Dictionary,* Oxford, 1933, vol. VIII, p. 1428.
7. See p. 13 below on the integration of the priest's professional roles of cultic, prophetic and ministerial offices.
8. See the *Apostolic Tradition* of Hippolytus, (www.bombaxo.com/hippolyytus/html) and *The Treatise on the Apostolic Tradition of St. Hippolytus of Rome*, Gregory Dix (1992). Notice also the organizational congruity of describing the community of God's people in terms of a democracy with the notion of the office of its hierarchical leader interactionally structured in terms of a trusteeship. See "On the Dogmatic Justification for a Process of Democratization in the Church," in A. Muller, ed., *op. cit.,* pp. 81–83.
9. See Gabriel Moran, *A Design for Religion,* Herder and Herder, New York, 1971, pp. 97–102. Notice that Moran defines education as "the improvement of human life through the devising of structures for learning" p. 146. The term "open education" is most significant for the purpose of drawing the ecclesiological role implications of Christian education. As this term de-emphasizes the authoritarian structures of teaching that close in on the classroom, it redesigns religious education on communal structures for learning that open into the environment. Its application to the problems of religious education in the institutional church is well-advised by the words of Herbert Kohl: "The development of open, democratic modes of existence is essentially the problem of abandoning the authoritarian use of power and of providing workable alternatives. That is a problem that must be faced by all individuals and institutions that presume to teach" (*The Open Classroom*, The New York Review, New York, 1969, p. 16).
10. It is evident not only from this study but also from the crisis of catechetics that more scientific research is critically needed in the areas of pastoral liturgy and religious education of children and adults. See the *General Catechetical Directory* of the Sacred Congregation for the Clergy, United States Catholic Conference, Washington, 1971, pp. 94–95. As this document suggests, "questions that have not yet been researched" must be probed and this would include exploring new ways of reorienting children in and even to the church. The missiological role implications of church membership in the light of current ecclesiology impel us to re-examine

the theology and to re-evaluate the liturgy of infant baptism. See my article, "Ecclesiology and Infant Baptism," *Worship,* 44:7 (1970) 433–437.

11. See G. Moran, ibid., pp. 97–120 and Ronald Goldman, Readiness for Religion, Seabury Press, New York, 1970, pp. 77–199.

12. Schell Silverstein, *The Giving Tree,* Harper and Row, New York.

13. Robert J. Lifton, *Boundaries: Psychological Man in Revolution,* Vintage Books, New York.

14. Gabriel Moran, ibid., pp. 96–120.

15. Richard McBrien, "The Necessary Ecumenism," *Commonweal,* 91:5 (1969) 145–148.

16. John Dunne, *The Way of All the Earth,* Macmillan, New York, 1972, p. IX.

17. Ibid., p. XI.

18. Ibid., pp. 224–225.

19. Ibid., pp. 220–221.

20. See Teilhard de Chardin, *How I Believe,* Harper and Row, New York, 1969, pp. 77–85.

21. Ibid., p. 85.

22. The plan would be constructed from the Parsonian theories on the institutional factors of interorganizational integration. See T. Parsons, "Suggestions for a Sociological Approach to the Theory of Organizations," in *Administrative Science Quarterly,* I (June, 1956) pp. 63–85 and II (September, 1956) pp. 225–239; see also note 1 of chapter 3 above.

References

Abbott, Walter, M., ed. (1966) *The Documents of Vatican II*, New York: Herder and Herder.
Alexander, Calvert, S.J. (1966) "Decree on the Church's Missionary Activity" (Ad Gentes) pp. 584–630 in *The Documents of Vatican II,* New York: Herder and Herder.
Argyle, Michael (1967) *The Psychology of Interpersonal Behavior*, Baltimore: Penguin Books.
Arndt, William F. and Gingrich, F. Wilbur eds. (1957) A Greek-English Lexicon of the New Testament, Chicago: University of Chicago Press.
Bales, Robert F. and Slater, Philip E.(1955) "Role Differentiation in Small Decision-Making Groups," in *Family, Socialization and Interaction Processes*, Talcott Parsons and Robert Bales, eds., Glencoe, Ill: Free Press.
Baum, Gregory, *The Credibility of the Church Today*, New York: Herder and Herder.
Bennis, Warren G. (1970) "A Funny Thing Happened on the Way to the Future," *American Psychologist*, 25:7, pp. 595–608.
Berger, Peter L. (1969) *A Rumor of Angels*, Garden City, NY: Doubleday.
Bishop, Paul (1966) "Pastoral Constitution on the Church in the Modern World" pp. 199–308 in *The Documents of Vatican II*, New York: Herder and Herder.
Bonaventure, Saint (1960) "The Tree of Life," no. 30 in *The Works of Bonaventure, Mystical Opuscula I*, Paterson, N.J: St. Anthony Guild Press.
Bresnaham, James (1970) "Rahner's Christian Ethics," in *America* 123:13, 351–354.
Brown, Raymond E. (1970) *Priest and Bishop: Biblical Reflections*, New York: Paulist Press.
Casey, William VanEtten and Nobile, Philip, eds. (1971) "The United States of America vs.The Berrigans: Some Documents,"; "The Indictment" and "The Response of 'The Conspiracy'" in *The Berrigans*, New York: Avon Books.
Cox, Harvey (1965) *The Secular City*, New York: Macmillan.
Curran, Charles (1978) *Issues in Sexual and Medical Ethics*, Notre Dame, Ind: University of Notre Dame Press.
———. (2013) *The Development of Moral Theology,* Washington, DC: Georgetown University Press.
Danielou, Jean (1964) *The Theology of Jewish Christianity*, Darton, Longman &Todd, London.
Davis, Charles (1967) *A Question of Conscience*, New York: Harper and Row.
Dewart, Leslie (1966) *The Future of Belief* : *Theism in a World Come of Age*, New York: Herder and Herder
Dix, Gregory, ed. (1968) *The Apostolic Tradition of St. Hippolytus*, London: SPCK. Dulles, Avery, S.J. (1966) "Dogmatic Constitution on the Church" pp. 14–96 in *The Documents of Vatican II*, New York: Herder and Herder.
Dunne, John S. (2011) *A Journey with God in Time*: *A Spiritual Quest*, South Bend, Indiana: University of Notre Dame Press.

———. (1972) *The Way of All the Earth*, New York: Macmillan.
Erickson, Eric H. (1963) *Childhood and Society*, New York, W. W. Norton.
Etzioni, Amitai (1968) *The Active Society*, New York: Free Press.
Faricy, Robert L. (1967) *Teilhard de Chardin's Theology of the Christian in the World,* New York: Sheed and Ward.
Fichter, Joseph (1968) *America's Forgotten Priests–What They Are Saying*, New York: Harper and Row.
Francis, Pope (2015) https://hbr.org/2015/04/the-15-diseases-of-leadership-according-to-pope-francis.
Freire, Paulo (1970) *Pedagogy of the Oppressed* , New York: The Seabury Press.
Gibbons, William J. ed. (1963) *Pacem in Terris* , Glen Rock, N.J.: Paulist Press.
Goldman, Ronald (1970) *Readiness for Religion* , New York: Seabury Press.
Greeley, Andrew (1967) "Principles of Personnel Policy," in *Secular Priest in the New Church* , Gerard S. Sloyan, ed., New York: Herder and Herder.
———. (1972) "The State of the Priesthood," in *The National Catholic Reporter* , 8:16 (Feb. 28, 7–10 and 15–17).
Grienacher, Norbert (1971) "A Community Free of Rule," in *Democratization of the Church* , ed. Alois Muller, vol. 63, pp. 87–107.
Guerrette, Richard H. (1970) "Ecclesiology and Infant Baptism," in *Worship* , 44:7, 433–437.
———. (1973) *A New Identity For the Priest: Toward An Ecumenical Ministry* , New York Paulist Press.
———. (1974) *The Re-Identity of the Priest: An Organizational Solution,"* in The Church as Institution, Part III: The Sociology of Ecclesiastical Institutions, Gregory Baum and Andrew Greeley, eds., Sociology of Religion, Nijmegen: The Netherlands.
———. (1981) *The Emmanuel Servant Community: A Case Study of a Social Movement Organization,* unpublished doctoral dissertation, London, Ann Arbor, MI: University Microfilm International.
———. (1986) *"Environmental integrity and corporate responsibility,"* Journal of Business Ethics, vol.7, 373–380.
———. (2015) *Management by Ethics: Innovative Discoveries for Corporate Ethical and Market Moral Reform* , Volume I, Lanham, MD: University Press of America.
———. (2015) *Ethical Theories and Moral Narratives in Art: A Gallery Tour through the Corporate Moral Forest* , Volume II, Lanham, MD: University Press of America, Hamilton Books.
Hall, Douglas T. and Schneider, Benjamin, (1969) *A Study of the Work Experiences and Career Growth of Roman Catholic Diocesan Priests* (unpublished manuscript) Department of Administrative Sciences, New Haven, CT: Yale University.
Hamel, Gary ed. (2015) "The Fifteen Diseases of Leadership According to Pope Francis," in *The Harvard Business Review* , (April 15, 2015).
Houtart, Francois (1965) *Sociology and Pastoral Care* , Chicago: Herald Press.
———. (1968) *The Eleventh Hour* : *Explosion of a Church* , New York: Sheed &Ward. Illich, Ivan D. (1970) *Celebration of Awareness: A Call for Institutional Revolution* , Garden City, pp. 69–94, New York: Doubleday.
Johnson, Robert Clyde, ed. (1961) "The Christian Ministry," in *The Church and Its Changing Ministry,* Philadelphia: The General Assembly of the United Presbyterian Church in the United States of America.
Kasemann, Ernst (1964) *Essays on New Testament Themes* , London: S C M Press.
Kittel, Gerhard (1965) *Theological Dictionary of the New Testament* , Wm. B. Eerdmans Publishing Co., Grand Rapids, Michigan, vol. III, pp. 763–764.
Kohl, Herbert (1969) *The Open Classroom* , New York: The New York Review.
Kottje, Raymond (1971) "The Selection of Church Officials: Some Historical Facts and Experiences," in *Democratization of the Church* , ed. Alois Muller, vol. 63, pp. 117–126.
Kung, Hans (1967) *The Church* , New York: Sheed and Ward.
———. ed. (1970) "Does Our Church Need a New Reformation?" in Concilium, Vol. 54, New York: Herder and Herder.

Lehmann, Karl (1971) "On the Dogmatic Justification for a Process of Democratization in the Church," in Concilium, *Democratization of the Church* (Concilium, Volume 63) New York: Herder and Herder.
Lifton, Robert Jay (1969) *Boundaries* : *Psychological Man in Revolution* , New York: Vintage Books, Random House.
Macquarrie, John (1966) *Principles of Christian Theology* , New York: Scribner.
Martimort, A. G. (1968) "Preliminary Concepts" and "The Structure and Laws of Liturgical Celebration" in *The Church at Prayer* , *Introduction to the Liturgy* , New York: Desclee, Co.
McBrien, Richard (1968) *Do We Need the Church ?,* New York: Harper and Row.
———. (1969) "The Necessary Ecumenism," *Commonweal,* 91:5.
McDonnell, Kilian (1970) "Catholic Pentecostalism," *Dialog* (Winter).
McKenzie, John L. (1966) *Authority in the Church* , New York: Sheed and Ward.
Mersch, Emile, S.J. (1951) *The Theology of the Mystical Body* , translated, by Cyril Volert, S.J., St. Louis, MO. and London, W.C. : B. Herder Book, Co.
Milhaven, John G. (1970) *Toward A New Catholic Morality* , Garden City, NY: Doubleday.
Moore, Wilbert. E. (1963) *Social Change* , Englewood Cliffs, NJ.: Prentice Hall.
Moran, Gabriel (1971) *A Design for Religion* , New York: Herder and Herder.
Morse, Chandler (1961) "The Functional Imperatives," in *The Social Theories of Talcott Parsons,* Max Black, ed., Englewood Cliffs, NJ: Prentice Hall.
Muller, Alois, ed. (1971) *Democratization of the Church* (Concilium, Volume 63) New York: Herder and Herder.
Nouwen, Henri, J.M. (1971) *Creative Ministry* , New York: Doubleday.
Ohlheiser, Abby (2015) "The 15 ailments of the Vatican Curia, according to Pope Francis," The Washington Post, December 22, 2014, https://www.washingtonpost.com/
Oxford English Dictionary (1933) Vol. VIII, Etymology of *profiteri* :"a public profession of faith."
Parini, Jay (2014) "Does Pope Francis Believe Christians and Muslims Worship the Same God?" *The Daily Beast* , December, 7.
Parsons, Talcott (1956) *Economy and Society* , Glencoe, Ill: Free Press.
———. (1956) "Suggestions for a Sociological Approach to the Theory of Organizations," Administrative Science Quarterly, I (June) pp. 63–85 and II (Sept. 1956) pp. 225–239.
———. (1967) *Sociological Theory and Modern Society* , New York: Free Press.
———. (1971) *The System of Modern Societies* , Engelwood Cliffs, New Jersey: Prentice Hall.
Poschmann, Bernhard, S.J. (1963) "Penance and the Anointing of the Sick" in *The Herder History of Dogma* , (Fr. Courtney, S.J. transl. Freiberg,-London: Herder-Burns and Oates.)
Pruyser, Paul W. (1976) "Lessons from art theory for the psychology of religion," (Presidential Address to the Society for the Scientific Study of Religion, Milwaukee, Wisconsin, October 25, 1975), *Journal for the Scientific Study of Religion* , vol. 15, no. 1–14.
Rahner, Karl (1963) *Theological Investigations* II, pp. 217–263, esp. 249, no.5, Helicon Press: Baltimore.
———. (1968) *Theology of Pastoral Action,* New York: Herder and Herder.
Schallert, Eugene J. and Kelley, Jacqueline M. (1970–1971) "Some Factors Associated with Voluntary Withdrawal from the Catholic Priesthood," *Homiletic and Pastoral Review* , 71:2–4, 95–106, 177–183, 255–267.
Schein, Edgar (1970) "The Role Innovator and His Education," *Technology Review,* 73:1, 32–38.
Schelkle, Karl (1965) *Discipleship and Priesthood* , New York: Herder and Herder.
Schumacher, E. F. (2010) *Small Is Beautiful* : *Economics as if People Mattered* , New York: Harper and Row.
Silverstein, Shel (1964) *The Giving Tree* , New York: Harper and Row.
Simms, Andrew (2015) "The Green Pope: How Religion Can Do Economics a Favour," *The Guardian* , June 18.
Teilhard de Chardin, Pierre (1965) *The Divine Milieu* , New York: Harper Torchbooks.
———. (1969) *How I Believe* , New York: Harper and Row.
———. (1972) *The Way of All the Earth* , New York: Macmillan.
———. (1964) *The Future of Man* , New York: Harper and Row.

Vogel, Cyrille (1982) *Le Pecheur et La Penitence dans l'Eglise Ancienne*. Paris: Cerf.
Williams, Colin (1963) *Where in the World*, New York: National Council of Churches.
——— . (1967) *A Question of Conscience*, New York: Harper and Row.
Williams, George H. (1956) "The Ministry of the Ante-Nicene Church (c. 125–325)," and "The Ministry in the Later Patristic Period (314–451)," in *The Ministry in Historical Perspectives*. eds. H. Richard Neibuhr and Daniel D. Williams, Harper and Brothers, New York, pp. 27–29 and 60–61 respectively.
Winter, Gibson (1966) *Elements for A Social Ethic*, New York: Macmillan.
——— (1961) *The Suburban Captivity of the Churches*, Garden City, NY: Doubleday.
Young, Guilford C. (1966) "Decree on the Ministry and Life of Priests" pp. 526–576 in *The Documents of Vatican II,* New York: Herder and Herder.
Zacharia, Fareed, (2015) Zacharia's Moonshots for the 21st Century, CNN 2/15/15).
Zayas de, Alfred and Dandan, Virginia, "United Nations Human Rights Experts Welcome Greek Referendum and Call for International Solidarity." United Nations for Human Rights: Office of the High Commissioner for Human Rights, Geneva, 30 June, 2015.

Author and Subject Index

Abbott, Walter: Vatican II Documents, 1, 2, 3, 6, 7n1–8n4, 14, 17n10–17n11, 28, 57n3, 58n8, 58n10, 59n20–59n22
Argyle, Michael, psychological interpersonal behavior, 53, 60n26
Arndt, William F., Greek New Testament Lexicon, 63, 78n3

Bales, Robert F., decision-making groups, 53, 60n26
Baum, Gregory, ecclesiastical credibility, 11, 47, 59n19
Bennis, Warren, G., a way to the future, 47, 58n16
Berger, Peter L., rumors and angels, 56, 60n33
Bonaventure, Saint, mystical works, 27, 32n16
Brown, Raymond E., liberal biblical reflections, 15, 18n16, 44, 47, 49, 58n12, 58n16, 60n30

Casey, William VanEtten, USA vs. the Berrigans, 21, 32n4
Cox, Harvey, religions in secular cultures, 54, 60n29
Curran, Charles, sexual and medical ethics, 65; developmental moral theology, 65

Danielou, Jean, Jewish Christianity, 16, 18n18, 21, 31n1

Davis, Charles, conscientious questioning, 11
Dewart, Leslie, theism and the future of belief, 74
Dix, Gregory, apostolic tradition, 14, 18n15, 67, 78n8
Dunne, John, journey with God; the way to God, 72, 74, 79n16

Erickson, Eric H., childhood and society, 12–13, 17n4
Etzioni, Amitai, active society, 55, 60n31

Faricy, Robert L., Christian theology of the world, 27, 32n18
Farley, Margaret, historical frameworks for sexual ethics, 18n17, 29
Fichter, Joseph, America's forgotten priests, 18n17, 29
Francis, Pope, identifying leadership diseases, 2, 19, 20, 42, 44, 60n27, 61, 65, 69, 74, 76, 77

Gibbons, William J., peace in the world, 31
Gingrich, F. Wilbur, Greek New Testament Lexicon, 63, 78n3
Goldman, Ronald, readiness for religion, 70, 79n11
Greeley, Andrew: personnel policy for priests, 29, 33n23; priests in the world, 38

Guerrette, Richard H., 5, 59n23; ecclesiology and infant baptism, 32n13; management by ethics, viii, 2, 13, 25, 32n13, 40, 48, 53, 57n1, 60n28; moral narratives in art, viii, 5, 48

Hall, Douglas T. and Schneider, Benjamin, work experiences and career growth of priests, ix, 4, 8n6–8n9, 17n9
Hamel, Gary, leadership flaws according to Pope Francis, 19
Houtart, Francois: sociology and pastoral care, 53, 60n27; transforming institutions, 53, 56, 60n27, 60n31

Illich, Ivan D., calling for institutional revolution, 47, 59n17

Johnson, Robert Clyde, changing ministry in the church, 63, 78n5

Kasemann, Ernst, New Testament themes, 21, 32n3, 44, 58n13, 58n14
Kittel, Gerhard, dictionary for the New Testament, 63, 78n4
Kohl, Herbert, the "Open Classroom", 68, 78n9
Kottje, Raymond, selection of church officials, 63, 78n2
Kung, Hans, new reformations: charismatic structures in the church, 10, 18n14, 33n22, 33n24, 58n13, 71

Lifton, Robert Jay, psychological man in revolution, 5, 70, 79n13

Macquarrie, John, principles of Christian theology, 18n15, 32n8
McBrien, Richard: new essence of Christianity, 9, 17n1; new theology of the church, 72, 78n1, 79n15
McDonnell, Kilian, Catholic Pentecostalism, 41, 58n9
McKenzie, John L., authority in the church, 10, 17n12
Mersch, Emile, S.J., mystical body of Christ, 26, 32n17
Milhaven, John G., new Catholic morality, 38, 40, 57n5, 57n6

Moran, Gabriel, improvement of human life, 68, 70, 71, 78n9, 79n11, 79n14
Morse, Chandler, imperatives for structural change, 54, 60n30
Muller, Alois, democratizing the church, 63, 67, 78n2, 78n8

Nouwen, Henri, J. M., creative ministry, 20, 22, 32n7

Ohlheiser, Abby, Vatican ailments in the Curia, 61

Parsons, Talcott: sociological theory of organizations, 13, 17n5–17n8; sociological theory and modern society, 35, 36, 39, 56, 57n1, 57n4, 60n26, 60n30; systems of modern societies, 25, 62, 79n22
Poschmann, Bernhard, penance and anointing the sick, 23
Pruyser, Paul W., the psychology of religion, 5

Rahner, Karl: theological investigations, 38–40, 57n5–57n6; theology of pastoral action, 10, 14, 18n13

Schallert, Eugene J. and Kelley, Jacqueline M., factors of priesthood withdrawal, 14, 18n13, 37, 60n32
Schein, Edgar, role innovation and education, 15, 18n17, 29, 32n21
Schumacher, E. F., economics and concern for people, 74
Silverstein, Shel, *The Giving Tree*: a caring ecology for people, 63, 78n2
Simms, Andrew, Green Pope: religion and economics, 75

Teilhard de Chardin, Pierre, liberal theology and conserving ecology, 22, 24, 27, 32n6, 32n11, 32n18, 61, 73, 74, 79n20

Vister Hooft, W. local life and the church, 41
Vogel, Cyrille, sinners and penance in the early church, 23

Williams, Colin: transcendent role of priesthood, 7; irrelevancy of the resident centered parish, 9–17n1; ecumenical directions for secular missions, 44, 58n11

Williams, George H.: ministry in ante-Nicean church, 16, 18n19; Ministry in Patristic period, 16, 18n19

Winter, Gibson: elements for a social ethic, 36, 57n4; ecclesiastical suburban captivity, 41, 52, 58n9, 59n25

Zacharia, Fareed: changing the gun laws of America, 67; earth sciences and the altars of technology, 70

Zayas de, Alfred and Dandan, Virginia, international solidarity and human rights, 75